El Salvado

El Salvador at a Crossroads

Salvadorans Speak Out About the War, Repatriation, and Their Hopes for the Future

Ralph L. Corrigan

Sacred Heart University Press
Fairfield, Connecticut
2014

Library of Congress Cataloging-in-Publication Data

Corrigan, Ralph L., 1937-
El Salvador at a crossroads : Salvadorans speak out about the war, repatriation, and their hopes for the future / Ralph L. Corrigan.
p. cm.
Includes bibliographical references.
ISBN 978-1-888112-21-4 (alk. paper)
1. El Salvador—Politics and government—1992- 2. El Salvador—Social conditions—20th century. 3. El Salvador—Social conditions—21st century. 4. Civil war—Social aspects—El Salvador—History. 5. Corrigan, Ralph L., 1937—Travel—El Salvador. I. Title.
F1488.5.C66 2014
972.84—dc23

2014009713

for Eilene

CONTENTS

PREFACE

In June of 1992, a group of faculty and administrators from Sacred Heart University in Fairfield, Connecticut, traveled to El Salvador six months after the signing of the peace accords that signaled the close of that country's brutal twelve year civil war. We met with *campesino* farmers, clergy, academics, women's rights activists, members of leadership councils, a high-ranking general in the Salvadoran Army, FMLN (*Farabundo Martí National Liberation Front*) combatants, rural healthcare workers, and workers in *cooperativa* projects, among others. Their stories form the core of this book.

Largely funded by more than four billion dollars from the U.S. Government, the war left the Salvadoran population raped and mutilated, with 75,000 dead, and villages obliterated under the "scorched earth" policies of the Salvadoran military operating under the High Command's directive to leave no witnesses. "I saw the shattered aftermath of such killing sprees: catatonic survivors, screaming orphans, the broken dead and dying," wrote James LeMoyne in the *New York Times Magazine* (February 9, 1992). "In a land named for 'The Saviour,' God seemed unusually cruel at times. The memory of such horror is likely to remain seared on the survivors for a generation or more."[1]

The peace treaty, signed in Mexico City in January 1992, ushered in an uneasy transition from open warfare to a hoped-for spirit of cooperation between government forces and FMLN guerrillas, but both sides recognized that serious obstacles to resolving their differences remained. These included the redistribution of contested lands in rebel-held zones, the dismantling of the rebel military apparatus, purging officer ranks of the army for war crimes, restructuring existing police forces, curtailing the activities of the right-wing death squads, and integrating the guerrillas and their leaders into a new political reality.

Observers believed that the army, facing the removal of officers from their ranks, might stage a coup, while the rebels, realizing that their armaments constituted a bargaining chip, refused to lay down their weapons. That was the reality upon our arrival in June of 1992. So why, given the fragility of the peace process at the time, did the administration at a Catholic university in New England decide to fund a delegation's trip to this war-ravaged nation?

To begin to answer that question requires visiting the campus back in the early 1980s, when a series of lectures sponsored by the university's Institute for Religion and Society honored Oscar Arnulfo Romero, the much-beloved Archbishop of El Salvador, assassinated March 24, 1980, while saying Mass at the Chapel of the Divine Providence in San Salvador. The lectures, including presentations by the poet Carolyn Forché and the peace activist Fr. Dan Berrigan, kept the university community informed of on-going atrocities in the country. Then, in November 1989, the assassination of six Jesuit professors at the University of Central America in San Salvador and their housekeeper and her daughter, shocked faith communities, campuses, and governments around the globe, igniting a firestorm of outrage and worldwide appeals to stop the civil war's horrific violence.

Sparked by this international call to action, a newly-revised mission statement promoting social activism, and the urge to support the efforts of Arturo Rivera y Damas, Romero's successor, the president of the university, Anthony J. Cernera, invited the archbishop to the campus to receive an honorary doctorate. It was during that convocation that the president committed the university to "a long term process of learning about and responding to the needs of the Salvadoran people." By the fall of 1991, the director of the university's Center for Ethic Studies, professor Gerald Reid, had drawn up a proposal for a faculty trip to El Salvador and forwarded it to the president.

Intended as a faculty development activity, it was hoped that the trip would provide colleagues with the opportunity to study, firsthand, Salvadoran educational and health-related systems, as well as emerging governing structures in a postwar Third World country. Another objective included laying the groundwork for faculty and student exchanges with a sister institution. And finally, the hope was that participants, listening to the stories of the Salvadoran people, would have their hearts opened and transformed and return home as ambassadors of social change.

With the president pledging support, twelve faculty and administrators came together to consider committing to the trip, and once the decision had been made to sign on we met weekly during the fall and spring semesters, reading accounts of the conflict between the American-backed ARENA (National Republican Alliance Party) forces and the five groups of FMLN rebels, and handouts on the social and political history of the country. We studied Spanish, were briefed by Minor Sinclair, our guide during our visit to El Salvador and the director of the Ecumenical Program on Central America and the Caribbean (EPICA), and by Fr. David Blanchard, a Carmelite priest, who spoke about his ministry with the repatriated *campesinos* of Calle Real outside the capital city of San Salvador.

"You will be amazed at the spirit of these people," Blanchard told us. "They have nothing. They don't even know where their next meal will come from. But they will greet you with open arms, and will go without food to prepare feasts for you. They are a warm, loving people. Nobody returns from a trip to El Salvador without experiencing life changes. The spirit of the people will affect you in ways you would never expect."

Our group which cut across colleges and disciplines, included Robin McAllister, a professor of English with a scholarly interest in Latin American literature; Maria Teresa Torriera, the founder and chair of the Spanish Department and advisor to the club *La Hispanidad;* Charlotte Gradie, a Latin American historian with a specialty in Colonial Mexico; Jose Ventura, a business management professor, interested in studying financial dependency issues in Third World countries; Gerald Reid, an anthropologist who worked with a Mohawk tribe in Montreal, and well-versed in the study of native history and cultures; Scott Willison, a professor of education, concerned about the welfare and schooling of children; Anne Barker, a professor in the nursing program, who hoped to study rural community health care practices; Dominick Sacco, a professor of criminal justice and a retired NYPD lieutenant, intent on discovering the progress on restructuring the Salvadoran police forces; Lauren Kempton, an adjunct instructor of education, who looked forward to studying the role of religious beliefs in the lives of the people; Eilene Bertsch, Assistant Vice-President for Academic Affairs, a trained sociologist and advocate of community service initiatives; Thomas Trebon, Academic Vice-President, charged with looking into developing student and faculty exchanges with a Salvadoran sister institution; Louise Spence, a film historian, who hoped to study the political and cultural dimensions of identity-formations; and myself, a professor of English.

What follows is a day-by-day account of the places we visited, the people we met, and the stories they shared with us, providing a glimpse of a moment in time when Salvadorans began to reclaim their lives, rebuild their communities, and look to the future. "Listen to their stories," Sinclair charged us, "observe as much as you can, then construct your own version of what happened here in El Salvador, so when you return to the U.S. you can bear witness to the struggles of these people."

In daily journals we jotted down personal reflections, bits of remembered dialogue, and descriptions of memorable events and scenes. And aware that we were listening to an oral history of events that took place during and after the civil war, we tape recorded the Salvadoran testimonies, spoken in Spanish and translated on the spot by Sinclair or Torriera, both experts in the language.

Latin American historians talk about the need to preserve first-hand accounts of Salvadorans who suffered the ravages of their civil war, and my hope is that this volume offers a partial response to that need. At the very least, after reading the testimonies, a person is free to make up her or his own mind about some of what transpired during and immediately after the conflict in the "Land of the Saviour." The appended glossary provides basic information about key terms, organizations, events, and people.

On a more personal note, what follows offers an overview of the actions and reactions of our group as we came face to face with a Salvadoran reality that spoke to our hearts. Fr. Dean Brackley, the Jesuit who traveled to San Salvador to take up the cause of his slain brothers at the University of Central America, said it best: "Just imagine what happens to you on a trip like this. Unless you are some kind of stone, these people, this reality, has the capacity, I think, to blow your world apart – to blow it away."[2]

I owe a sizable debt of gratitude to the folks who helped sustain my sporadic efforts over the past twenty years or so to guide this book toward publication.

First, thanks must go to colleagues who traveled to El Salvador in June of 1992, at a time when the country was in the throes of post-civil war turmoil. Special thanks go to Gerald Reid who proposed the trip and guided the rest of us through that first visit.

Much thanks to Minor Sinclair, our patient, knowledgeable guide, who made sure of our safety, supplied us with much-needed commentary along the way, and herded us through a crowded schedule of interviews and visits to rural and urban communities.

Thanks also go to professors Charlotte Gradie and Gary Rose for reading the final manuscript and encouraging its publication. And I'm grateful to professors Robin McAllister and Joe Myers for their help translating Spanish passages on wall murals and etched over the entrances to buildings.

I am grateful to Deborah Dutko for her expert work on the cover design, using photographs taken by Eilene Bertsch, Robin McAllister, Gerald Reid, and Thomas Trebon.

A load of thanks must also go to Eilene Bertsch, for her support during our first trip to El Salvador, and for her prodding and unflinching encouragement to see this book in print. She's a "treasure."

To my colleague and longtime friend, Sid Gottlieb, I can truthfully say this volume would not exist without his encouragement and expert editorial advice. His eye for detail, his gentle suggestions, and his enthusiastic support made working with him a joy.

And last but not least, my gratitude goes to Judith, my artist wife, who makes all things possible.

Ralph L. Corrigan
Professor Emeritus
Sacred Heart University

Chapter One

Mirna's Welcome

"I want to give you the welcome of this small country. It is a country that is so interesting because of what is happening right now while you are here."

Flight 885's cabin lights dimmed crossing the shoreline of south central El Salvador, San Salvador volcano jutted into the clouds in the distance, and below farmlands fanned out in a green patchwork of squares and rectangles. To the right the Rio Jiboa snaked northward from the Pacific Ocean through the Department of La Paz, and from several thousand feet in the air the land, only a few short months earlier held hostage by a vicious civil war, looked peaceful and prosperous.

As the jet slipped down toward Aeropuerte International an on-board radio crackled and sputtered with names – President Alfredo Cristiani, General René Emilo Ponce, General Mauricio Vargas, and rebel leaders Joaquín Villalobos, Shafic Handel, and Ana Guadalupe Martinez. The names I recognized, but the Spanish commentary was lost on me. Was the cease-fire unraveling? A coup taking place? In the seat next to me a well-dressed Salvadoran woman nervously fingered her rosary.

Then the wheels touched down and the Salvadorans on board broke into applause, laughing, shaking hands, slapping each other on the back. They had come home. But to what? The woman, relieved to be on terra firma, sighed, scooped up her beads, dropped them into her purse, then joined the queue in the aisle, while outside on the tarmac soldiers with assault rifles scrutinized the disembarking passengers. With the guerrillas demobilizing less than twenty percent of their forces, and rogue elements of the Salvadoran Army and police forces swelling the ranks of the death squads, the soldiers were under orders to provide airport security.

Inside the terminal we waited in lines to pass through Immigration while a trim uniformed woman seated in a glass enclosure motioned for us to step forward one at a time.

"What is the purpose of your stay in El Salvador?"

"I'm with a university delegation, here to study the situation after the signing of the peace accords."

"I hope you have a pleasant visit," she said, smiling as she stamped the visa page and handed back the blue booklet.

Downstairs, Minor Sinclair, sporting a black cap with a large white "X" over the brim, was waiting by the baggage terminals, a grin on his face. A guide for several U.S. delegations in El Salvador in the past, he had spent the past week or so in the country making last-minute adjustments to a packed schedule of interviews and community visits.

After locating our luggage we followed Sinclair out to the parking lot where we met our driver, Romero, a compact *campesino* with a round smiling face, a thin moustache, and dark, short-cropped hair.

"We'll take the old road to the hotel," Sinclair announced as we piled into the van. "I want you to see some of the countryside. It's a much better introduction to rural living conditions."

— 2 —

Turning off the main highway to San Salvador, we followed a mountain road twisting and climbing through a rugged volcanic terrain of rocky rises and drops covered with dense vegetation. Shacks, cobbled together with sheets of black plastic and corrugated tin roofs, peeked out from under canopies of trees, and barefoot, half-dressed children, mothers in peasant dresses, and men in work clothes and straw hats, stood in dirt yards along with chickens and pigs, or peered out of doorways as we lumbered by. Along the side of the road women carried bundles of firewood, canisters of water, or baskets of fruits and vegetables, and men, machetes in hand or swinging from belts, walked along herding cows or goats.

"Stop here," Sinclair said by a group of roadside stalls. "Anybody hungry? You have to try a *papusa*."

Instantly, half a dozen women, baskets on their heads or under their arms, hurried across the road, surrounding the van, jostling for position, shouting at us to buy drinks, ices, fruits, and nuts. We purchased snacks, and the women, encouraged by a few sales, shouted louder, thrusting items through the open windows. At that point a light rain interrupted the pleading women and they retreated across the road.

"Check out the *papusas*," Sinclair said, gesturing toward several makeshift shacks while he and Romeo tied a large tarp over the luggage on the roof.

We hurried across the road and ducked under a shed roof where a woman in a flowered print dress and white apron was cooking patties of dough on a large skillet over a fire.

"They're corn tortillas filled with refried beans and cheese," Sinclair explained, joining us.

The woman scooped dough out of a black basin, kneaded it, patted it flat with her palms, and plopped it on the skillet.

"You all should try one," Sinclair said in his Southern drawl. "Get your first taste of an authentic Salvadoran food staple."

The *papusas* smelled inviting, felt warm and soft, and tasted delicious.

— 3 —

Passing into the city, Romero drove up the Bulevard de Los Heroes past a huge soccer stadium, then turned right on Alameda Franklin Delano Roosevelt, a main thoroughfare in the capital. Exhaust fumes hung in the stifling late afternoon heat, Latin music blared from radios and loudspeakers, and cars and pickup trucks packed with people and hanging off the sides, whizzed past horns honking.

Blocks later we turned right and parked in the entryway of the Alameda Hotel, hoping for a good night's sleep before setting off to visit rural communities in Usulután in the south central part of the country. Inside the lounge was filled with suitcases and packs, plastic covered chairs, and a sofa facing a large TV. To the left, glass doors opened into the *Bar Cavalier* and *La Mansion Restaurant*. It was five o'clock.

"Why don't you get situated in your rooms," Sinclair said. "We'll meet back down here in the lobby at six for supper. That should give us plenty of time for showers and to get your stuff together. There's a place down the street with tables outside and it serves good food. And remember, dress conservatively. You don't want to draw attention to yourselves."

Dominick Sacco, my roommate, and I, lugged our gear up to room 418, which came with two twin beds, a desk, a bureau, a couple of chairs, and a bathroom with shower. A large window overlooked a pool in the rear courtyard, and a tray on the bureau held a pitcher of water and two glasses.

Around six our group trickled down to the lobby.

"It's called a conservative way of dressing. Oh yes!" quipped Maria Torriera, pointing to Lauren Kempton decked out in baggy harem pants decorated with large colorful squares, lines, and circles.

"I told Maria this is my most conservative outfit," she said. "She doesn't believe me."

Hungry after a day of traveling, we trooped out of the hotel, turned right, crossed Franklin Delano Roosevelt Avenue at the end of the block, then walked a short distance to the *Cafe de Don Pedro*.

"It's noted for its Salvadoran food," Sinclair said, herding us past tables packed with dinner patrons.

On the sidewalk in front of the cafe a young boy carrying a basket filled with bouquets walked back and forth, crying out to the diners to buy his roses. At the same time, an older man hawked postcards.

"It looks like we're going to have music with our meal," said Sacco, gesturing toward two men dressed in Mexican costumes and sombreros, one with an accordion, the other a guitar.

A waitress took orders for drinks and handed us each a menu. I looked over the items in Spanish, and couldn't make any sense out of it. The fact was, in our group Torriera, Ventura, Gradie, and McAllister spoke fluent Spanish; Kempton, Willison, Reid, and Sacco, sticking to basics, could read a bit and manage to make themselves understood; but Barker, Spence, Bertsch, and myself let the others do the talking.

Drinks ordered, along with entrees of *papusas, empanades, and chorizes*, we settled back to enjoy the two men serenading the patrons. Then halfway into the meal, Sinclair stood up saying he had to leave to pick up the speaker for the night's session. "I'll be back in twenty minutes," he said, "so finish eating and take some time to relax."

When Sinclair returned he introduced Mirna Anaya, a short, stocky woman with dark hair, and her daughter Gloria. Mirna, he explained, was a lawyer and wife of Herbert Anaya, one of the founders and former president of the non-governmental Human Rights Commission of El Salvador [CDHES], assassinated outside his home October 26, 1987. Active in the FMLN, he worked on the committee for the disappeared, was jailed for nine months in 1986, tortured, and was the fourth leader of the Human Rights Commission killed in the 1980s.

"We'll meet back at the hotel," Sinclair announced. "I'll go back with Mirna and her daughter and try to get a room for our orientation meeting. If you want to stay here and enjoy the atmosphere, that's fine. Or you can take a walk, but be sure to stay together. And don't go down any side streets."

The avenue's evening traffic had thinned, and Gradie, McAllister, and I decided to take a short walk. At the time I couldn't help wondering what the people we passed on the sidewalk thought about three *gringos* strolling along. Did they question who we were, or why we were there? I couldn't tell. They seemed to ignore us.

Teenage boys lounging on the corners and in front of stores brought to mind Sinclair's earlier warning about youths on the streets. "They can cause trouble," he had said.

Then as we were walking down the avenue, suddenly Gradie stopped. Ahead of us stood two military personnel with assault rifles.

"I'm not going to walk past men carrying guns," she said.

We looked at her.

"I don't like guns."

— 4 —

Our meeting in Room 409, set up to serve as an introduction to the current situation in El Salvador and scheduled for 7:30 that evening, started closer to nine.

"The eulogy Mirna delivered for her husband in the National Cathedral in San Salvador," Sinclair said, "was one of the most moving speeches I've ever read."

Surrounded by her five children at the altar, Mirna had said:

> People of El Salvador, a thousand times heroic!
>
> At this time, so filled with pain and grief by separation from my husband, I thank you for being here. You feel as I do, and as so many of our people who cannot be with us today feel. You gave my husband the opportunity to voice your suffering and your anguish. Without you, he would not have been what he was. He was humble, and you inspired him to give his life for all of us. You gave him courage by your example.
>
> I also thank everyone who has come from outside the country to share in our suffering. I thank you for your demonstration of solidarity with my family and the Human Rights Commission. I want to remind you that our people continue to suffer. They need your support. You must continue to lift up your voices to denounce the oppression. I repeat the call of Archbishop Romero. I plead with those

> of you who are members of the security forces. Stop killing your brothers and sisters. We are poor, just like you. Stop this killing!
>
> I do not ask for vengeance against those who assassinated my husband. Herbert never hated them. If he could speak today, he would forgive them. But he would also demand, with the same courage that he always demonstrated, that they stop killing their brothers and sisters.

A *cri de coeur*, Mirna's eulogy begged for healing to begin.

To start the meeting, Sinclair suggested we say a few words about our initial impressions of El Salvador. "Just what strikes you about the country. Anything you have to share."

"When we arrived," began Reid, "I was overwhelmed. Then when the plane landed, all the Salvadorans clapped. I wondered if they were coming back to El Salvador."

"I expected more misery, more signs of the war," Torriera added.

"A little girl was selling peanuts along the road," said Kempton, "and we said no. The little girl sighed. It was such a desolate sadness." Then she asked Mirna, "Could you explain the term *mística?*"

"I think it means 'of the spirit.' It is an energy that comes from the *pueblo*. A sense of the people. Maybe that's what you call *mística.* And that means to work without seeing that things will get better. And that is why the people who are dead are not dead. They are still alive. This is something that helps me to understand the mystery of the Resurrection. People who have died ten years ago or three years ago are still alive. In fact, they are working harder today."

"Herbert told a nun that when he died she would see a rose on her desk. Before she even heard of his death, she saw a rose in a garden. A rose in a garden means death. But the rose goes beyond death. In its essence, it means life. The spiritual power that the people have goes beyond. Maybe it is the sign of the rose that calls you to something great. To feel the strength of the Salvadoran people. To feel the *mística.*"

Then Mirna talked about how in the early days of the war the women left their children to work for the movement, and how people in First World countries called them irresponsible. "But the situation here was so critical," she said, "and of such profound crises, that people did things that under normal circumstances would not be possible."

With that said, she launched into her prepared remarks.

Mirna Anaya's Testimony

I want to give you the welcome of this small country. It is a country that is so interesting because of what is happening right now while you are here. It is a moment in time when we can find out how much political space we have been given by the peace accords. And now is the time to work.

We are a people who have been forced to leave our country. We've met many people, good people. But the right to live in your own country is what brings all of us back. I could live anywhere. But after living for four-and-a-half years outside the country, I've learned a lot.

This is a special time because of the peace accords, but we still have many problems. According to the peace accords, the National Guard and the Treasury Police are supposed to be cut back and disbanded, but the killings still go on. The government movement to set up the National Police, supposed to have started at the end of April, has not started yet. As a result the FMLN has not abolished more than 20 percent of its forces. Both sides were asked to concentrate their men in special zones. The FMLN is in twenty camps, the government forces are in sixty-seven.

The war has ended because there are no military fights at this time. But the death squads are still operating. One nun was decapitated. But that is part of the cost. A special

Truth Commission has been formed to study the military and to tell who killed and who was killed. And that work is very important.

Four point four billion dollars from the U.S. kept the war going. Secretary of State Aronson and Baker saw that they couldn't win the war, so they made some changes. But in this country, there will be no real changes in the power structure. Just in the past eight days, neither the army nor the FMLN has reduced their forces. They have not made any drastic changes. If there was an outbreak tomorrow, both forces would be at full strength.

One of the reasons to end the war was because of the business community. They were saying that the war must end. During the last ten years, the business community went to hell. But still a lot of people made a lot of money during the war. Especially the military. They now have enormous pension funds set up for themselves. The army is still the strongest power in the country. So if the officers have to go away, then they feel it has to be made worth their while.

The five armies of the FMLN have developed themselves into a political party, and they held an open demonstration ten days ago. Just a few years ago, to speak of peace was considered subversive. And with the ability to speak out comes a lot more support from the people. Such talk was suppressed for so long, and now the people can come forth and talk about the war.

A negotiated settlement. That's what people call it. But both sides will have to give in, and the social struggle will be very strong.

When she finished, Sinclair outlined our upcoming schedule, and our plan to visit the community of Hacienda California the next day.

"You are going to a community that is one of the most important examples of what is happening here," she said. "I got to know these people in 1977 through the work of my husband Herbert. He worked with the people, selling their homes in Chalatenango when they left for Nicaragua. And now these people are returning to El Salvador."

Finally she mentioned the upcoming celebration at the Gerardo Barrios Plaza in front of the National Cathedral for the FMLN war-wounded returning from Cuba.

"We'll all be there. For the leadership of Hacienda California to be able to go to the rally is a new experience for us. Just a short while ago these people could have been killed for attending such a thing."

She ended the meeting by saying, "We are going to be a land of tremendous conflict."

Before leaving the room Sinclair reminded us to ready our gear for the next day. "Everybody pack so you are carrying only one bag. Just bring whatever you will need for an overnight," he said. "Expect this to be primitive."

Primitive or not, it didn't matter. As Eilene Bertsch had said earlier, "I felt like I wanted to do anything to make this trip happen."

— 5 —

Four months after we left the country, the Brigada Maximiliano Hernandez Martinez death squad, intent on saving their country from domestic and foreign meddlers, issued the following communiqué on October 22, translated by the Christian Urgent Action Network on El Salvador [CUANES]:

Death to the Terrorists

> Since the signing of the nefarious and unconstitutional Mexico accords with the terrorists of the FMLN, inconceivable acts have occurred in our beloved country, and if we don't stop it once and for all, lamentably we would not be responding as men, but as children.

> The situation is already intolerable to know that as a product of this accord with the terrorists our glorious armed forces will be cleansed, our National Guard dissolved, the terrorists will keep our land and are also controlling the new PNC [National Civil Police].
>
> The country has been invaded by pseudo-communists foreigners the white pestilence of ONUSAL [UN Observer Mission, El Salvador]. If things continue like this, in 1994 the red and green communists will take power and this we will not allow to happen. El Salvador is for the Salvadorans and we must defend and struggle for all or nothing. For all the above reasons, the patriots organized in the commandos' Brigada Maximiliano Hernandez Martinez communicate the following:
>
> Come October 31 we will proceed to accomplish a death sentence on all the terrorists – Joaquín Villalobos, the Turkish assassin Shafik Handal, Ana Guadalupe Martinez, Jorge Melendez, Salvador Samayoa, Facundo Guardado, Jose Alberto Ramos, Chano Guevara, Leo Cabrales, Fidel Fecinos, Eduardo Sanchez, Marco Jiminez, Nidia Diaz, Francisco Jovel, Leonel Gonzales, Salvador Gurra, and all the other terrorists responsible for the tragedy our country is living.
>
> And also we state that the white pestilence of ONUSAL must leave, and so too the foreign journalists that have invaded our country. All the national journalists, the traitorous politicians, the front organizations, and all those who collaborate with the terrorists. All those must accept the consequences from the liberating national justice.[3]

Two months later Mirna herself and her children came under attack. The February 1993 issue of *Centroamérica* ran the story under this headline: "Five Killed, Mirna Anaya Attacked."

> Mirna Perla de Anaya, vice-president and former general coordinator of the Central American Human

Rights Commission (CODEHUCA), was attacked by gunmen while traveling with her family in El Salvador on January 3. After stopping the Anaya vehicle with a red, police-type light, six masked men fired a dozen times, wounding Miguel Ernesto Anaya (age 15) in his right side.

Anaya's assailants fit the description of members of a government anti-drug unit who attacked a resident of "Ciudadela Guillermo Ungo," a repopulated village, at the end of December.[4]

CHAPTER TWO

SR. ELENA AND TIERRA BLANCA

"This is how we get the word out."

"I am the Mother Superior," Torriera announced at breakfast the next morning in the hotel dining room. "Does anybody have to take their malaria pills?"

"I have worry dolls for everyone today," Kempton joked, showing off her earrings.

"That's fine," someone quipped, "unless someone cuts your ears off."

That comment was not far off the mark. It reminded me of a prose poem by Carolyn Forché read by my students. Written in 1978 during events leading up to the war, the poem explained what happened when she was invited to dine at the home of a Salvadoran colonel:

> Broken bottles were embedded in the walls around the house to scoop the kneecaps from a man's legs or cut his hands to lace. . . . I was asked how I enjoyed the country. . . . There was some talk of how difficult it had become to govern. The parrot said hello on the terrace. The colonel told it to shut up and pushed himself from the table. My friend said to me with his eyes: say nothing. The colonel returned with a sack used to bring groceries home. He spilled many human ears on the table. They were like dried peach halves. There is no other way to say this. He took one of them in his hands, shook it in our faces, dropped it in a water glass. It came alive there. I am tired of fooling around he said. As for the rights of anyone, tell your people they can go fuck themselves.[5]

Shocking words, shocking images, met with expressions of disbelief on my students' faces.

The morning schedule called for a stop at Tierra Blanca, a Christian-based farming community in Usulután administered to by a nun from California, to be followed by a visit to Hacienda California, a sprawling farm coöperative currently in the hands of the *campesinos* who took control of lands they had worked on after the owners fled in the early years of the civil war.

"The farm of about twenty-five hundred hectares was run by the Palomo family," said Ventura, who had seen a letter written to Sinclair outlining the cooperative's recent history. "When the family left the farm in 1980, the *campesinos* started to farm the land."

After listening to Mirna the night before, and her hopes for the future of her country, this excursion promised to be an opportunity to test her belief that now, for the first time, people were beginning to feel free to talk about their past history, about how the war affected their lives, and what they thought the future might bring.

Outside the hotel, the morning traffic on Franklin Delano Roosevelt Avenue was again in full swing with a cacophony of noise from honking trucks, buses, cars, motorcycles, and scooters. A red pickup truck careened past with at least twenty kids standing in the back and hanging off the sides waving and laughing.

"There's no school," someone announced.

"They're probably on some kind of excursion."

"The teachers are on strike," said Sinclair. "They're asking for better working conditions and more money. Others think the education of the young people should come first."

—— 2 ——

Sinclair asked Romeo to swing past Casa Clementina, a small restaurant in San Salvador, to pick up Teresa, a young mother working as a waitress who needed a ride to Hacienda California.

Then we drove south from San Salvador along the four-lane highway and turned east through LaPaz, El Rosario, and Santiago Nonuaclco.

Near the small village of San Marcos we crossed a one-lane bridge over the Rio Lempe where women standing ankle-deep in the muddy water washed small piles of clothing, dunking items then rubbing them on flat rocks.

About a quarter of a mile past the bridge, Romeo pulled over and parked in front of the San Marcos Market, a collection of shacks and small cinder block buildings.

"Time for a stretch," Sinclair announced. "You can buy sodas and snacks here."

At the first shack a woman, surrounded by family members, held a small child on her lap. The child was sick and Barker, the head of our university nursing program, went to investigate.

"She has a fever," she explained. "She needs attention. This is frustrating, because if the child doesn't get to a hospital, she could grow sicker and die."

We were told that the mortality rate for children under the age of five in El Salvador was roughly four times greater than in the U.S. Sadly, in the case of the small child, Barker's hands were tied.

Back toward the river, power lines ran along the road, and in a fenced in area several cattle grazed, and beyond, set back from the road, was a building with the sign "*Base Militar San Marcos Lempa.*"

"That's for the military personnel maintaining the security of the bridge," Sinclair said. "So it doesn't get blown up. Bridges were prime targets during the war."

By the base two white oxen, a heavy wooden yoke behind their horns, pulled a rickety cart with thick, mud-encrusted wooden wheels onto the road. The driver, a young man in a white T-shirt and dark pants, sat on a wooden box holding two ropes tethered to the oxen in his right hand and a long stick in his left. Behind him a young boy holding onto an upright pole in the cart's platform, stared at us as the rig creaked by, the oxen's hooves clopping on the pavement.

— 3 —

After leaving the market, we drove a short distance down the road, and turned right toward the village of Tierra Blanca, the home since 1988 of Sr. Elena Jaramillo of the Sisters of St. Joseph from Orange, California. We pulled up in front of a white stucco wall with a ramp leading through a large entryway. "*Iglesia Nuestra Señora de Guadalupe*" [Church of Our Lady of Guadalupe] was painted in large letters to the left of the entryway along with a life-size portrait of the Virgin, on the other side was a large heart in dark blue with a cross on top.

Romeo steered the van through the entry, parked in the courtyard, and we followed Sinclair inside the community church, where several children sat on benches by the entrance cutting out paper hearts. Nearby a woman recited prayers with another group of children.

White plaster walls, large grill-like windows, and rows of wooden benches faced the sanctuary where an immense wooden cross with a life-sized Christ figure and paintings of the Sacred Heart and the Virgin dominated the rear wall.

We stopped to say a prayer, then Sinclair led us outside to a triangular courtyard where we sat on benches and chairs under shade trees waiting to meet Sr. Elena.

At that point someone brought up Sinclair's warning about the "primitive conditions" at Nueva Esperanza.

"What about sleeping conditions?"

"You don't do a lot of turning in a cot."

"Would there be some sort of shelter?"

"We're their guests," Sinclair remarked. "They'll do their best to accommodate us."

"When we talked to that mother about where she could take that child," Barker said, "I wondered if we were going to see the hospital?"

"That's in the city of Usulután. It's a city of ten to twenty thousand people. But it's not on our schedule."

"The child doesn't probably need to see a doctor right now," she added. "She doesn't need help until 'mal grande.' "

— 4 —

By way of introducing the small, trim woman standing next to him with sun-darkened skin and close-cropped gray hair, Sinclair said, "Sister Elena does a tremendous amount of good pastoral work with displaced people at some risk to herself, and with a lot of love."

"Welcome," she said. "The community is anxious to have you visit. They are delighted to have visitors because this is how we get the word out. And I'm sure you are wondering what I do here. I've been here for five years. Tierra Blanca numbers about six thousand people, with many of the *campesinos* farming the salt works."

"The salt works?" someone asked.

"Salt water from the ocean runs into concrete patties the workers constructed," she explained. "The sun evaporates the water, leaving the salt to be collected. But the salt is not being harvested right now because of the rainy season. And there are problems. Certain people are putting pressure on the buyers not to buy the salt, or to buy it at lower prices. For example, salt sells for sixty colones for a one hundred pound sack, and our people could only sell it for fourteen colones. Buyers from Guatemala came about ten times, but because of pressures placed on them not to buy, nothing was sold."

"We're talking about raw, unprocessed salt," said Sinclair. "The farmers want to process it, but that calls for another level of industry."

"Recently, the workers rented a mill where they hoped to iodize the salt," said Elena. "But finding buyers remained an issue. It was just one more example of the power of the elites. They could apply pressure anywhere they wanted to stymie the efforts of the *campesinos.* And what better place than to let the farmers do all the work, then apply pressure so they couldn't sell their product."

This, she said, was a classic ploy of people in power, the wealthy landowners hiding behind the law and elected officials, to keep the poor in their place while lining their own bank accounts.

"The farmers want to produce shrimp as well," she added. "So some of the patties are used for that purpose. The workers plant the larva, then in nine months the shrimp can be harvested."

The bottom line for Elena was to break through the cycle of *campesino* poverty by developing a life-sustaining economy at Tierra Blanca. "I'm working with a group of women, and I've explained to them about working together as a collective."

By now it was getting late and we had to leave for the farming cooperative, but not before we visited a project close to Elena's heart, her garden.

"I'm working with people on a medicinal garden to make all kinds of medicines," she said. "We maintain a large medicine chest and sell the medicines. Each person who prepares the medicine makes about fifteen cents on a bottle. Our interest in natural medicines and herbal ingredients grows directly out of the fact that regular healthcare is inaccessible and too expensive. So we contract to have a natural herbal medicine group come out here, and the doctors don't seem to pooh-pooh the natural medicines."

Then Elena talked about the health clinic she started at Tierra Blanca.

"There is a clinic that the people can come to. I say, 'Look, I am not a nurse. But let's look in the book and see what it says.' We have the book called *Where There Is No Doctor*, by David Warner, and another book that tells us about fifty plants from Honduras. The book has the names of the medicines, then the names that the native people use, and then the uses of those medicines. Basically, taking care of people's medical needs becomes a team effort."

— 5 —

In this out-of-the-way community of war refugees in Usulután, Elena struck us as a perfect example of someone living out the gospel of administering to the needs of the poor. With her quiet sensibility, her welcoming smile, and a "let's get to work" way about her, she had found her life's calling – bringing order and civility into a badly battered world

"Remember how she would walk," said Bertsch years later, recalling her first impressions of Sr. Elena. "There was a silence. There was a strength about her. When she walked through the community I felt she was almost not touching the ground."

Also at the time, there was no way for any of us to know that our visit to Tierra Blanca would jump start a long-term relationship with Sr. Elena and the people she served – a relationship that eventually brought her to our campus in Connecticut for an honorary doctorate, and which for years to come would include visits over Spring Break by student delegations who worked on community projects and fell in love with the people, especially the children.

After Sr. Elena extended to us an invitation to return to Tierra Blanca for lunch, we drove to the entrance of the Hacienda California cooperative and discovered a closed barbed wire gate and an armed guard.

"The leadership of La California is supposed to be expecting us," Sinclair said. "Maybe communications got mixed up."

He got out of the van and walked over to the guard, explaining who we were. The man must have understood because he nodded, unlocked the gate, and motioned us to pass through.

"There was some trouble here just a while ago," Sinclair said, climbing back into the van. "It seems the owner arrived with the Hacienda Police to take back his property. This happened when the farmers are trying to buy the land to form a cooperative so they can determine their own destiny. When the contingent of police approached the gate demanding entrance, word spread quickly, and the farmers rushed from working the fields, massing in protest behind the gate. They were carrying machetes, hoes, stones, and whatever else they could get their hands on. It was a classic David versus Goliath match-up. When the two sides faced each other, the battalion of police withdrew to the other side of the road opposite the gate. Tensions mounted, but the farmers refused to budge, saying they would fight to the death for the land. Eventually, to avoid another massacre, the police left and the workers celebrated their victory."

Beyond the gate we drove past vast fields stretching into the distance, and finally arrived in front of the farm's *finca* [house], parking under a grove of trees. Romero shut off the engine and suddenly several men in combat fatigues brandishing rifles surrounded our van.

CHAPTER THREE

APOLO AND LEONIDAS

"The army killed my mother, my father, my uncles, and sixteen cousins."

"I don't know what this is all about," Sinclair said, surveying the men outside. "Stay inside the van. I'll find out what's going on."

He opened the door, jumped out, and the men crowded around him. Sinclair is tall. We could see his face above the others, and as he tried to explain yet again who we were and why we were there, the men started to nod their heads.

Then Sinclair slid open the side door of the van. "This is a group of guerrillas who have come to support the cause of the local *campesinos* here," he said. "Don't worry. They are friendly. I told them that you do not agree with the policies of your government, and that you have come to support the peace efforts."

At that point a few of the men ambled off toward the *finca* , which we later learned served as their command center, while others stood or sat in the shade under the trees. One young man – about eighteen years old and dressed in a ragged uniform – studied us as we stepped out of the van, as if he wasn't sure what to make of us. He was thin and wiry, with a rifle slung over his shoulder and a frown on his face.

Meanwhile Sinclair stood talking to one of the farmers, a broad-faced man with squinting eyes, a thick black mustache and beard, dressed in work pants, a T-shirt with a red FMLN insignia, and wearing a wide-brimmed straw sombrero.

"He says you can walk around behind the *finca* to take a look at the guerrilla encampment," Sinclair said. "And if you want to, you can check inside the building."

Palomo's old residence, built on a dirt-filled platform held in place by a three-foot stone wall, consisted of a main floor and a large attic with two dormers. The front windows were shattered, the front wall blackened by smoke, and over the front entrance a crudely painted sign announced "Asoc. Coop. Prod. Agrop. La California." A makeshift awning of straw was propped on wooden poles over the entryway, and next to the door another straw roof covered a stone table and broken chair. Piles of wood, discarded furniture, crates, and plastic pails were strewn along the sides of the house.

Behind the *finca*, about two dozen guerrillas lounged under the trees while others moved in and out of the main building. That was when Sinclair came up with an intriguing idea.

"Would anyone care to talk to the group of *Norte Americanos* about the conflict?" he asked. "It would be an opportunity for a group of international visitors to hear about the war from the perspective of a combatant."

After some discussion, a young man stepped forward, agreeing to talk to us. He led us around the *finca* under a canopy of orange and mango trees filled with squawking birds to a wood-framed structure with picnic tables and a tarp roof.

"These people are teachers and administrators scheduled to be in El Salvador for ten days," Sinclair began. "They have been preparing to meet with the people of El Salvador for the last ten to twelve months. While in the country they will be visiting several communities and the universities. But mainly they have come to learn about the recent history of El Salvador and the current situation, so they can return to the United States and tell their colleagues and students what they learned."

"With the hope of being some assistance in your struggle," Willison added.

The young combatant introduced himself as "Apolo," and said he was the leader of this contingent of men. Jose Ventura described the scene:

> We are introduced to a young man, not thirty yet, trim, 5 and ½ feet, maybe 150 lbs. He wears boots, his

pants are ripped, his T-shirt is also not of recent acquisition. The pants are olive-green, the color that many people in this country have worn for many years. He seems not sure of his role today. He does not look people in the eye, his hand grip is not very strong, he is nervous, as a matter of fact he would smoke very much, one cigarette after the other. But he is a very important person as we would later learn. He is the leader, the guerrilla leader, and he was not supposed to be there. In fact, while we were there we heard some airplane engine noise and men from his unit carefully came out to look where the airplane was. As the engine noise got louder and louder, they would disappear, making sure that they would not be observable from the air. Under the densely covered trees, or disappearing into the house, they just did not exist.[6]

— 2 —

Apolo's Story

We are a small group of FMLN and we should be some distance from here. But the government is not complying with the peace accords, so we are here to support this community.

Q) With families, did some children join with the FMLN and others join the government forces?

A) That happened a lot because of forced registration. Others would join the guerrillas. People from the same family didn't see each other. But now after the cease fire, we can see each other without being on opposite sides.

Q) Can you integrate easier with the police forces because of the peace accords?

A) It depends on the guidelines followed and the training of the police force. If the accords are rigidly adhered to, then everyone could join.

Q) Can you tell us a little bit about your personal history?

A) I am from the Department of Morazán. We all saw that there was a real need to join together because of the rich people who controlled the wealth of the country. The poor people tried to make progress little by little, but they did not have any freedom of expression. Only the wealthy. There was no democracy for the poor.

So years ago the people started to protest. The labor unions took to the streets, and the response of the government was to repress these groups. So there were no other options than armed struggle. And that was the case that was shared by so many people, the labor unions and others. We had to fight to survive.

In the early years of the war the government policy was to exterminate the people who lived in areas where the guerrillas were. There were massacres. And at that point, when we saw what the army did, people began to realize that the FMLN was part of the struggle of the people, and so the FMLN became more powerful. The idea was to force the government to negotiate. Maybe it was more of a bluff, but the FMLN continued to press until the negotiations could be held. And that is where we are now.

There were two of us in the family, and in 1980 we saw the need and joined. After my brother and I collaborated with the FMLN, then the repression hit. The army killed my mother, my father, my uncles, and sixteen cousins. Given that, we had no choice but to confront the army. What happened to my brother and my family happened to so many families. And in many places the government armed forces lost the support of the people.

Q) We are now in the cease fire, but when do you and your people think peace will occur?

A) In the past ten years there has been no liberty or freedom or justice. And now we see this transition period. We feel if the agreements are carried out as they are supposed to be, there will be peace. Peace is where there is real democracy, and where there is freedom.

Q) Did you expect problems with the compliance of the army with the accords?

A) We anticipated this before the agreements were signed. Negotiations started with the former Christian Democrat Napoleon Duarte, but they were not sincere. The same happened with the ARENA policy. They would share dialog, but not negotiate. The truth is, there are two armies in this country.

At first, ARENA did not want to accept that the United Nations had a role in this peace process and the whole issue of a UN presence here. The government was against this. But the FMLN said the UN must be here or nothing will happen. We know that signing the agreements and putting them into practice are two different things.

We foresaw the problems before they arose. There are elements within the military and the wealthy class that would not comply with the accords because it was not in their best interests. The armed forces, for example, did not concentrate in areas where they were supposed to be. They were in twenty areas more than where they should have been. So we hold five areas where we are not supposed to be.

Also the land has traditionally belonged to the very wealthy. And the rich say, "We will not give up our land." This is a big hacienda owned by Joaquín Palomo. People have come here who were displaced by the war and they built small shacks. But the owner says he will not sell the land. We feel he has no choice. He must sell. And so we have an obstacle to the peace.

At issue is that part of the peace agreement about lands in the conflictive zones. We believe these lands should be available for purchase by the people who live there and work the land. But the problem was that if the owners didn't want to sell, then they didn't have to. So the FMLN talked to the owners, and then more people were willing to sell their lands.

> Q) What will you do if peace comes to your land?
>
> A) Looking at the basic people of our army, if the agreements were complied with, some would become part of the National Civil Police, some would move into production, others would join the political process as part of the FMLN party. For myself, I would like to study more. So far, I've completed the ninth grade.

When Apolo ended his presentation, we thanked him for talking to us, and as he walked back toward the *finca* we could not believe we had just heard the testimony of a guerrilla leader.

"The behavior of this young man moved me tremendously," Ventura said. "He is a young man in a hurry, driven to do something for his people."

How long the rebels would camp at the *finca* was anybody's guess.

— 3 —

Shortly after Apolo left, five members of the cooperative's leadership council joined us. Dressed in shirts, long pants, and straw hats, the farmers, serious expressions on their faces and speaking in measured tones, introduced themselves and their roles in the cooperative.

"Maybe you could tell us a little about the history of the community," Sinclair began. "But maybe we shouldn't start too far back."

Leonidas, a short, wiry man, with a sun-tanned, angular face and a bushy black mustache, wearing over-sized aviator-style glasses and dressed in a faded work shirt and dark pants, spoke for the group.

Leonidas's Story

> Through the 1970s the hacienda had about three thousand employees. People worked together at that point. And the owner of the place, Joachim Palomo, assigned

people to work in different areas. He also had supervisors or overseers. We were paid two colones to work from seven in the morning to four in the afternoon. That would have been about fifty cents a day. We could earn that wage if we were able to finish what we were assigned to do.

For example, we would work in this *finca* here where the plantation house is. There are lots of orange trees here. The daily work assignment would be for one person to dig three holes per day to plant the orange trees a meter wide and a meter deep. But the soil was very hard, and we would dig and work all day and only be able to dig one hole. It would take us three days to earn the wages for one day, because we didn't complete the one day's assignment. So the wages of fifty cents were spread over three days.

I remember in the '70s when we were working here digging these holes, and the mango trees that are still here were here then, too. Sometimes the mangos would be pecked by the birds and they would leave only the shell. Well, one of our workmates was walking by here, and there was one of these mangos on the ground. It really had been pecked to death. There was just a little piece of mango still in the shell. He picked it up and for stealing that mango he was penalized two weeks. He was laid off for two weeks.

When they gave out the payroll that Saturday, they paid the workers the money for the past two weeks, and said publicly, "You've been punished for stealing mangoes and you will be suspended for two weeks' work because everyone knows you don't steal fruit from the hacienda, the big house." The punishment for being laid off for two weeks meant a lot of hunger, because there was no other work.

While that happened to the worker, at the same time Palomo, who lived in this house, had this tremendously big dog from the United States. When that dog barked, you could hear it up in the town of Tierra Blanca. And when they fed the dog, they would slaughter a calf every two days to get meat to feed it. The workers, seeing this kind of injustice, began to organize. It started first in the salt works. Workers began to protest and demand that the wages be raised, and the work requirements for the day to be fair, something that we could really do in one day's work.

Then the repression started. Right at the end of this road, you may have seen it coming in, there was a National Guard Post. There were four National Guards there, maintained by Joachim Palomo. They patrolled the whole area mounted on horses with G-3 pistols in their hands.

They came to where we were in the salt works and asked us, "Where are your ID documents?" The people who had been involved in the protest were pulled aside, and written up by the National Guards. And they decided what to do with them. There was no prison for protesting workers. They would capture somebody, take him away, and the person would be "disappeared." This caused panic within our working unit. And so when people were taken away in front of everybody, the fear got to the point where no one would recognize what he had witnessed. No one saw anything because he feared that the same thing could happen to him.

To give you an idea of the fear that the people had and the repression, about a thousand meters from here, maybe a quarter of a mile, there is a well and there was a family that had been "disappeared" by the National Guard, and their bodies thrown down that well. The remains of the family are still at the bottom of the well. To spread more fear, peons working here at the hacienda would be dragged from their houses in the middle of the night and killed and thrown down wells or disappeared. No one would know where they were. We began to see what a massacre this was. The people who were captured never came back. Many of the *campesinos* didn't have any other option but to go to the mountains.

"This," Sinclair interjected, "is generally a reference to joining the guerrillas."

And also, groups of *campesinos* would begin to come together, go out in the streets, and protest. In 1980 the *campesinos* had real political power, which they showed that year. One way they showed their power was in marches. Here within the hacienda they went to the stables where they milked the cows and burned and destroyed those stables. There were three stables. One of seven hundred cows of two milkings a day, another of six hundred cows, and another one hundred cows used for regeneration purposes. Those stables were burned to the ground and destroyed. This year was when the army began to mobilize and grow to be a giant army.

Q) How many of the people, all the people, or just a small group of people, were doing this?

A) About half the workers. The other half were dead or had fled to the mountains. Everyone that remained. And so when the army began to mobilize and hold military operations, there was some conflict, some skirmishes between the guerrillas and the army. Joaquín Palomo, at this point, left the hacienda. He couldn't work because there was too much fighting. He couldn't exploit the workers in the same way. Many had left, and those who stayed were organized and would not do the same kind of work. And the other reason was because the war here was in flames, and there was fighting and crossfires, and he couldn't stay here himself.

From 1980 to 1987 was a real hard part of the war. At the end of 1987 we organized for the first time an initial cooperative here. This was really done at the behest and the initiative of a regional federation of cooperatives which, incidentally, was pro-government. The leadership committee of the cooperative was bought and manipulated by Joaquín Palomo. The president of the cooperative obeyed the orders of Joaquín Palomo. Every member of the cooperative who farmed two acres of corn had to pay four hundred pounds of corn to Joaquín Palomo. And that continued into the next year, 1988.

By 1989 people realized that we had to restructure this cooperative. Everyone who was working then realized how unjust it was to pay any of the little profits that were there to Joaquín Palomo. He would come, bring his big trucks in here, load up with our corn and leave, and at absolutely no cost to himself.

So we realized we had to restructure and we had meetings to set that out. We reformed the *cooperativa* based on formal procedures. And when Joaquín Palomo realized that the *cooperativa* had been restructured and that his representative here at the hacienda was no longer a part of the committee, he turned to other forms of control and repression. He sent one battalion of the army, nine hundred and fifty soldiers, to be based in this whole area.

They were sent here, they said, by the High Command, and that they had orders that we didn't have any rights to live or to work here. They threatened us that they were going to force us out, or they would arrest us and send us to prison. But we held strong and we didn't lose our position.

When they forcibly tried to evict *campesinos* from their homes, we had to respond with our own organization. We organized demonstrations and marches at the Sixth Brigade of the army in San Marcus Lempa to show that we were strong and that we were united. When Palomo realized that the army would not evict us, they began to act on legal cases through the judge there to arrest leaders from the cooperative. There were arrest warrants out for eight members of our leadership council. But this didn't move us. We continued to work.

Then they sent another man, a man named Roberto Larios, the brother of Colonel Larios. He came saying that he had rented the land from Joaquín Palomo and it was his to use. Then he went to the salt works and worked there for about four months during the dry season.

We didn't like the fact that he was working in the salt works because we felt the salt works were part of the larger cooperative and it belonged to us. We began to think, how can we get him out of there? But it was hard because he was a very wealthy and powerful man. He also continued to have a military presence here. It was like a military detachment of the Coast Guard.

We went down there and he was there with all his soldiers. He had a nine millimeter military pistol in his belt, an armed weapon he used to threaten the workers with while they were working. When the people from the cooperative would go out into the ocean and fish, they would catch these minnows and come back with them. Larios would send the army to take those small fish from them and throw them back. The people were really upset because that was going to be their food for the day.

This was part of the confrontation when we were down there, and most of the people were scared and left. All that remained were the thirteen members of our leadership council, Larios, and his military people. We began to say, "This is an injustice which you are doing to our people." They got really angry. We began to discuss this, and argue with the officials of the army who were there. It was a very heated discussion. That day we made the decision that we would not let him work the salt works. In ten days, he came back and met with the cooperative with an agreement to work for Larios for ten colonnes a day.

Larios complained to the Auxiliary Bishop of San Salvador, and we were invited to a meeting in the Cathedral. At the meeting, Larios performed very well. He seemed like an angel, but we said to his face all the things he had done to us.

We were supposed to have a second meeting here, but he put an article in the paper saying we had stolen his workers. Then he started a court case against the thirteen leaders. On January 30th, the day before they signed the peace accords, the military entered the cooperative, looking for the President and Vice President of our committee to force us off the salt works. They said, "Either these two go back to the city with us, or we will force everyone off the salt works." The two men were held twenty-one days in captivity.

Laws in our country are bought and sold with money. Larios bought the judges. All the money we had paid through fees was used against us. We'd seen this before, and we asked for help from the other cooperatives. We organized eight truckloads of *campesinos* and we took over the courthouse and began to negotiate with the judge who was the local Attorney General. The Attorney General agreed to enforce the law if the judge would not. And so with his presence we loaded ourselves back on those big trucks and went to Usulután to the department capital with the Attorney General. And when we were in the chamber of law, we demanded that that judge be removed. And we achieved that. The next day he was removed. The next day we went and we got our two *companeros* back out of jail.

Since then, as the leadership council, we've been able to rest a little bit because we haven't had the same kinds of problems that we had in the past. Maybe that gives you some idea of what is at issue.

— 4 —

"Would members of the leadership council be willing to accompany us for the rest of our visit to the hacienda?" asked Sinclair. "That might give us a better chance to ask questions about production and how you organized. Is that agreed?"

The council members nodded yes, then Leonidas agreed to answer questions.

Q) When half the men were taken away, and were disappeared, and there was great fear in the cooperative, how did the men then come together and face that fear and begin to work together, without the fear that they too would be taken away?

A) We are talking about two groups of people. Those who fled and those who stayed with panic. Part of the way we overcame the panic is that we said we had to organize and defend ourselves, and when we found the means to defend ourselves, we began to take more courage in order to calm the fear. And part of it was to get a few .22 and .38 caliber pistols. Then people began to develop more connections with the revolutionary organizations and the guerrilla armies who would give them more of a sense of being protected. And that is how the people overcame their terror.

There were also those who left. I was one of those who left. My situation was that my work here in the cooperative was not with machetes to work the land, but I had other kinds of work to do. It was very serious. And when they found out about the work I was doing, the National Guard came to my house and asked questions. I happened to be in San Salvador at the time and realized I was being sought after, so I fled to Honduras. Others were in different situations, like parents with small children, and their option was neither to stay nor to join the guerrilla organization because of their situation. But many left the country. They are the ones who now would be called the "returnees" or the "repatriated" refugees.

Q) What about healthcare here?

A) There is none. The hospital is too far, the nurse too expensive, and no physicians are available. If one gets sick, one dies.

Q) Do you really believe that peace is coming?

A) I'll tell you why I am confident, and that is because we are *campesinos*. In El Salvador, millions of us are

> *campesinos*. We have power. We'll go into the street and demonstrate. We can rely on ourselves and our organization. And that gives me confidence that there will be peace. We think peace is fundamental to being able to develop our communities and to develop our cooperative. It is a fundamental requirement.

The meeting over, we left the picnic tables and walked back toward the *finca*.

"I have never heard anything like this before," Sinclair said, shaking his head in disbelief. "And it is because of the new situation in this country. Before the signing of the accords, the people's fears of reprisals were so great they were unable to talk freely about their experiences and concerns."

Near our van, three guerrillas in combat fatigues, sleeves rolled up, were resting under a tree. I grabbed my camera, and held it out for the men to see, but I couldn't tell from their expressions if they minded having a picture taken. Bivouacked where they were not supposed to be, with no real idea who I was or what might be done with the photo, they must have had second thoughts about the situation.

When I snapped the shutter, the youngest of the three stared directly at the camera, the second guerrilla raised his arm, hiding his face, and the third, his face badly scarred, turned away.

Chapter Four

La California and the Salt Works

"Can campesinos purchase land?"

"There is much contention over this point," Jose said. "Palomo could not return to the old ways. That is not feasible now. And secondly, the farmers who occupy the land are willing to work the land to pay for it. But it will take time."

It was after one o'clock when Sinclair called us together.

"We could go in the van and visit the salt works," he said, "or we could stay where we are and visit the school and other facilities. Sister Elena is planning lunch for our group back at Tierra Blanca. But since I didn't expect us to interview an FMLN combatant, we're running a bit late on our schedule."

The school was a priority, but after Leonidas's description of the stand-off between Larios and the *campesinos* at the salt works, I needed to see the place. All I could picture was a flat expanse dotted with piles of white salt.

Most of the group elected to stay, including Torreira, charged by the Spanish Club at the University to adopt a Salvadoran elementary school. "They all agreed that I should choose the most needy school," she said.

Sinclair, McAllister, Sacco, and I drove off in the van with the president of the cooperative, Jose Santos Duran, a stocky *campesino* with a round face, dark mustache, and goatee.

We followed a dirt road south toward the coast, and as we curved past corn fields and through wooded, marshy areas, questions about Leonidas's talk surfaced. For example, how did the leadership handle folks who opted out of the day-to-day grind? I asked Sinclair to put the question to Jose.

"*Campesinos* try to help one another when a member is sick or hurt and not able to work," he answered. "People pick jobs they are suited for, and they earn money for their labor. People who do not work so hard earn less."

"What if someone steals something?"

"If that happened it would be put to a vote, and he could be asked to leave."

"Can *campesinos* purchase land?"

"There is much contention over this point," Jose said. "Palomo could not return to the old ways. That is not feasible now. And secondly, the farmers who occupy the land are willing to work the land to pay for it. But it will take time."

— 2 —

When we pulled up in front of a one-story wood building around 1:30, the community's center of operations for the salt works, half-a-dozen *campesinos* sat on the front porch eating lunch. Window screens, metal drums filled with trash, wheelbarrows, and plastic buckets littered the ground, and to the right in a clearing a pile of salt bags baked in the sun.

Across from the shack, rectangular pools of water, roughly 25 by 75 feet, stretched into the distance almost as far as the eye could see. Ditches carrying sea water from the coast ran alongside pools edged by two-foot-high brick walls. Past the salt works a thin line of bushes and palm trees bordered a grassy area, and beyond rose the dark angular peaks of Usulután. To the south, the sun's reflection off the ocean turned the mid-day sky a pale blue.

"A recent storm damaged the salt works," Jose explained, as we followed him to the ponds. "Retaining walls have to be rebuilt, and the muck in the bottom of the pools cleaned out."

He stopped momentarily by a pool, its flat bottom covered with reddish-brown silt.

"We flood the pools with ocean water, seal them off, and the water is evaporated by the sun. Then we scoop out the salt by hand to be bagged."

At that point McAllister strolled off with one of the workers, balancing on the brick walls, the two of them making their way across the pools until they were specks in the distance. Meanwhile, Sacco and I walked over to inspect the bags of salt in the clearing by the shack.

Crystals on the ground escaped from the sealed bags looked chunky and cloudy, and larger than the fine, white, processed salt back home. Curious, I popped one in my mouth. It tasted brackish.

When we drove back toward the hacienda, McAllister, in the rear seat, was still talking with his *campesino* friend.

Later I asked him, "Robin, what did you talk about?"

"Oh, nothing much."

I didn't believe it. I had read and admired his travel writings, and was sure he was collecting details for an essay on El Salvador.

— 3 —

Near the hacienda our group was standing with folks from the cooperative in the shade of huge trees bordering a large soccer field where a spirited match, with the spectators shouting encouragement, was underway.

Reid and Willison, invited to play, accepted the challenge, but only after some good-natured ribbing about their general fitness. Still a bit jet-lagged, they nevertheless joined the younger players on the field, intent on trying to put on a good show.

Already late, we waved goodbye to the people under the trees and drove off toward Elena's for lunch. It was 2:30.

En route, talk about the elementary school dominated the conversation. It turned out that over two hundred children attended six grades with a staff of two teachers in a dilapidated school building with holes in the roof.

"I thought it was a chicken coop," Torriera said. "It was a small wooden building, without divisions, just a very large room in very bad condition. Many of these children's mothers, like Teresa who came with us from San Salvador to La California, work in the capital to earn money and only on free days can come home to see their families."

"What's their future?" Bertsch asked. "What do these children have to look forward to? I just don't see much hope for them. They will grow up and experience the same subsistence standard of living as their parents."

As a footnote, upon her return to the States, Torriera, recommended the Spanish Club adopt the school at La California, and in the following months, *La Hispanidad* raised money to repair the roof, mailed boxes of educational materials, and collected over one hundred pairs of children's shoes (a requirement for attending classes).

Summing up the overall situation for the farming cooperative, Sinclair said, "Here there is some hope for poor farmers, but only because they benefit from the support of the FMLN."

But across the country, negotiations between the government and the *campesinos* taking over the farms they had worked on, sometimes for generations, stood at a standstill. Insurgents, filing land claims after the conflict, said they would lay down their weapons when several hundred thousand acres, amounting to roughly 12 percent of El Salvador, were turned over to their families and sympathizers. But facing shortages of money and pressure from wealthy landowners to reclaim their farms, the Cristiani administration was banking on the rebels to scale back demands.

On the road toward Tierra Blanca Sinclair pointed out a house with an adjacent ten foot square concrete pillbox, the same fortification mentioned earlier by Leonidas. During the hostilities, as a safety precaution, Palomo had it built as a National Guard command post. Three feet of the squat building stood above ground level, with gun turret slits cut into the sides.

"The pillbox is attached to the house by an underground passageway," Sinclair said.

"FMLN" was scrawled on the walls with orange paint, and on the other side of the road two young boys, oblivious to the menacing-looking bunker, played with sticks in the dirt.

— 4 —

When the front doors to Sr. Elena's compound swung open, Romeo drove into a courtyard and parked in front of the church. In the open area under trees where we had met Elena earlier, women were preparing our meal, and it was close to three o'clock by the time we sat down to chicken and rice.

"So get used to it!" Sinclair said, laughing.

After we finished, one of the cooks took it upon herself to instruct us on the proper way to clean plastic plates. She motioned for us to follow her to the well area where she picked up a dish, scraped the chicken bones and leftovers into a large plastic pail, then wiped the dish clean with a soapy cloth in one basin, rinsed the dish in a second basin, and set it down to dry. As we washed our dishes and finished cleaning up, she stood nearby eyeing us critically. At that point sounds of strumming guitars wafted across the courtyard, and as we walked toward the music, I glanced back over my shoulder. The woman was rewashing our dishes.

In Elena's office, Willison and a young girl sat on chairs facing each other, cradling guitars, he strumming background chords, she plucking away on the melody and singing the lyrics.

"I want to get close to the people and immerse myself in the culture," Willison announced, looking up as we entered the small room. "Hey, that's what we're here for. Right?"

In a rear room over a desk hung a framed wall poster of Oscar Mensenor Romero with a group of young girls in white dresses holding banners and flags, with a quote in block lettersthat read, "*Si me Matan, Resucitaré en el Corazon del Pueblo Salvadoreño*" ["If they kill me, I'll be reborn in the heart of the Salvadoran people"]. The words referred to Romero's "spirit of the martyrs" speech in March of 1980, just before his assassination. "As a Christian," he had said,

"I don't believe in death, but rather in Resurrection. Martyrdom is a blessing that I don't believe I deserve. But if God accepts the sacrifice of my life, let my blood be a seed of liberty, and the sign of hope will be a reality."

Against the rear wall, two locked metal cabinets with glass doors held jars and small plastic containers.

"These are their medications," Barker said, trying to decipher the labels.

Stacked neatly in rows, the contents of the medications, written in Spanish in a tiny script, remained a mystery.

Invited by Elena to view the medicinal garden she mentioned earlier that morning, we trooped outside, walked past the front of the church to a plot approximately an eighth of an acre in size, guarded by a five-foot concrete block wall topped with barbed wire fencing.

"We have to protect the garden from thieves," she explained.

Expecting an intricately laid out plot, I was surprised to find what appeared to be a patchwork of grass, bushes, and weeds.

"To the right," she said, "is the section for the medicinal herbs."

Surely the leaves of these plants would be vibrant yellows and deep purples and reds. Instead, the shrubs looked scruffy and ordinary, plants you would pass in the woods without giving them a second thought.

The garden tour over, we thanked Elena for hosting the lunch, promised we'd return, and headed south to the community of Neuva Esperanza, bouncing over pot holes and ruts in a dirt road lined on either side by trees and brush, passing women balancing baskets and jugs on their heads, and men with machetes in hand or slung from belts, and small herds of plodding cattle, haunches and ribs showing, tended by boys carrying long sticks.

"The machete is an apt symbol for the Salvadoran struggle," McAllister commented. "It serves the dual purpose of a farming implement as well as a weapon of defense."

"Ah, the men are treated as gods," Torriera countered. "So we let them think so."

Romeo braked to a stop on a small rise where the dirt road sloped down to a muddy stream. On the other side was the settlement. It was about 4:30.

"I scheduled Nueva Esperanza early in our stay for a number of reasons," Sinclair explained. "First, so you can experience how the people of a repatriated community live and work while trying to create a viable life in spite of the government's attempts to undermine their success. Second, to listen to the stories of the community leaders so you can better understand their views about the war, their repatriation from Nicaragua, and the role of the government in their relocation. And finally, so you can witness firsthand the spirit and solidarity of the people as they struggle to survive."

Since the community's recent founding, he added, members had constructed temporary housing, dug wells for water, set up a school and infirmary, planted crops, laid out an area for a cattle farm, and worked out a community-based governing structure.

Braced with that information, we hefted our gear and trudged along the dirt road down to a narrow wooden footbridge where we crossed the stream and hiked up the road on the other side to a large signboard that read: "*Bienvenidos a la Communidad Nueva Esperanza*" ["Welcome to the community of Nueva Espernza"].

Past the entrance, shacks made with long wooded branches, plastic sheeting sides, and corrugated tin roofs, lay scattered under mango trees on either side of the dirt road.

Chapter Five

Soledad and Nueva Esperanza

"There are no historians left in El Salvador. They were assassinated during the war. So the history of contemporary El Salvador is to be discovered in the stories of the people."

We stopped in front of a nearby shack, and Sinclair explained to a man that our group was expected, and would he tell someone from the leadership council we had arrived, and that we apologized for our lateness. The man walked off, returning minutes later with a pixyish-looking woman with a thin, sharp face, her hair in a pony tail, dressed in a tan skirt, pink blouse, and wearing sandals.

"Soledad recently returned from lecturing in Germany," Sinclair said, introducing her. "She told about the history of her people and about her experiences in the civil war. She was soliciting aid for the community."

"There are so many teachers here," she said, surveying us. "And we don't have any at all."

"International visitors to Nueva Esperanza help support the efforts of the people to achieve a new life," said Sinclair. "Their mission is to relate the history of their recent struggles. Your job is to listen to their stories, to observe as much as you can, then construct your own version of what has happened here in El Salvador, so when you return to the U.S. you can bear witness to the struggles of these people."

Soledad led us under the trees to the left of the entrance sign to a rectangular one-story bunkhouse. Inside were three square rooms, roughly fifteen by fifteen feet, with dirt floors and walls of rough planking. The first two rooms, reserved for workers, were furnished with four cots covered with blankets, clothing, and personal belongings. The room at the far end of the bunkhouse, reserved for visitors, held four more cots – one covered with books and clothing, another with mosquito netting, and two more against the end side wall. Soledad instructed us to leave our packs on the empty cots.

"We'll figure out who will sleep where later," said Sinclair. "We're going to another building where some of the community leaders will tell us a little about this place and their personal histories. But before we go there, Soledad has asked if any of you would care for a soda and some fruit."

With that, Soledad led us to the community canteen where we crowded around a long wooden counter, ordering bananas, sodas, and packets of saltines.

Sinclair had explained earlier that food and lodging expenses had been paid for. "We try to make a generous donation," he said, "because these people have so little."

Snacks in hand, we followed Soledad to a large pavilion that held a scattering of desks, chairs, small tables, and benches. Grain sacks marked "*Producto USA*" were piled on a platform at the far end under a banner announcing in large red letters: *Por la Paz y la Vida-Communidades Unidas* [For Peace and Life, the Communities United]. A white rooster, perched high on top of the sacks, cocked its head from side to side.

We sat in a circle at child-sized desks and were soon joined by a man with long dark hair, a mustache, and small goatee, wearing jeans and a T-shirt. On the T-shirt was the picture of a man's face which later Sinclair said was a commandant from Nicaragua.

"There are no historians left in El Salvador," Sinclair said, getting the meeting started. "They were assassinated during the war. So the history of contemporary El Salvador is to be discovered in the stories of the people. Many stories can be told for the first time because the signing of the peace accords diminished the terror of retribution in the minds of the people."

"It is not our fault, what we say," Soledad said, "because it is the truth. Your visit gives us courage because it comes from the heart."

Soon another man arrived and sat next to Soledad, introducing himself as Pilar Martinez. "I'm a member of the community and a construction worker."

"And I work in the area of internal communications," Soledad added.

— 2 —

Soledad's Story

I'll try to share some of the history of our community, and although you probably wouldn't get all of the details, with two or three people taking part, maybe we will get much of the story out.

As Juan indicated, we are really happy you are visiting us here to see how we live because we don't live as people live in San Salvador. And the government is partly to blame for that because in 1980 they scorched us out of our homes. It was a policy back then, a policy of "scorched earth." That means no living thing survives in that field.

I lived in Chalatenango, and the army came through and burned our house. They came through and burned our crops. When they came, we would leave the house and go hide in the bushes and the mountains. I had a girl who was born underneath a tree while we were fleeing. That happened again and again to us.

And in 1980 there was a massacre at the Sampul River, which you may have heard of. On that day, the army corralled the people and forced them ahead at gunpoint to the mouth of the Sampul River where they committed that great massacre. The River Sampul was right on the border. The Salvadoran Army fired down from one side of the river, and the Honduran Army fired from the other side of the river, and those who didn't die by being shot were drowned in the river because it was already flooding because of the rain storms. It was more than a tragedy. On my mother's side we lost fifty family members. Six hundred people died altogether, not to mention another seventy people who died and were never found.

But we are a people who really believe in God, and that faith has kept us united, and kept us with hope to the point where we are today. And so we saved all the things we could, and then we went to the Red Cross and asked for help. They took us to a refuge in the basement of the Church of San Roche in San Salvador.

When we arrived there we were out of our minds. The army came there when we arrived, and they circled the church, and they cut off all food coming into the church. And there were six hundred people living in the basement of this church. They were sleeping on the floor, and there was a single bathroom in the church that we shared among us. There was no room for us in the church because it was already overcrowded, but we had no other place to go. Finally we were allowed to join the others in the basement.

One morning the toilet flooded and we were in the basement and it caused a tremendous problem and we were trying to clean that up and the military came in and started beating and harassing the people. Three times they forced their entry into the church and captured and disappeared two people.

We lived with a lot of anguish during that time. I lost my father there. He was with us, and he got sick, and the Red Cross came and took him to the veteran's hospital, saying they would bring him back when he was better, and he disappeared. We never saw him again or heard what happened.

In the church, it was always one thing after another. First an epidemic of typhoid, then a measles disaster. We never were able to feel good living in the basement. But one thing we always remembered though was the four North

American church workers, who were actually the four women who were killed on the highway. They helped us whenever they could, and they would get all that they could raise and sneak it through to our community. And another person who was very important and played a very big role was a Jesuit priest, Joachim, who was killed recently. And then of course, the Vicar General of the Archdiocese helped us to get out of that situation.

At the time there was a man from England, a guy named Julian, who helped us to get asylum in Nicaragua. And when we got to Nicaragua as refugees there was a big party. They celebrated our arrival. And we came with just the clothes on our backs.

The Sandinista government in Nicaragua received us very openly. They gave us land to work, and so Salvadorans began to farm. They gave us loans for agriculture, they donated a tractor, they gave us a truck, and we were able to buy small tools for agriculture, and a plow. We had everything there. But we kept asking ourselves, when are we going back to El Salvador? Throughout this whole war it was always when can we go back to El Salvador? There was always the war, but El Salvador was the first thing on our minds.

In 1990 something very strange happened. We were reading a text in Jeremiah, and something jumped off the page, and it said, "They left crying and returned in happiness." And it said in the text, "I will enable you to return to your land now." It was like it was a God-send.

So when we were talking we began to question ourselves again, saying well why don't we go back? We're Salvadorans, and we have a right to go back to our own country. And we began to take the initiative of doing a survey among the Salvadorans in Nicaragua to begin to see if they wanted to go back. And if they wanted to go back, did they want to go back on their own, individually, or did they want to go back in a big group, organized? All of the people who wanted to go back said, "We want to go back in community."

After we began to make an appeal to the United Nations Commission for Refugees, they said that they would make the appropriate request to the government, the Salvadoran government. What they were saying was the problem was that we had chosen to go to a country where there was a revolution, and because of the revolution we would not be able to return to our country. The accusation was that we belonged to the FMLN, and that's really what the main gist of it was.

We said, "If we belonged to the FMLN we would be there with rifles in the mountains. We wouldn't be in exile with our children."

Then the government changed in Nicaragua, and we went through a whole wave of harassment, of pressure by the new government against the Salvadoran refugees. The elected Chamorro government published a list of the Salvadoran guerrillas who had been nationalized in Nicaragua, with first and last names. And that list was a signal for the death squads from El Salvador that were now in Nicaragua to take care of the problem.

We set up a small office in Nicaragua to help get Salvadorans organized to return. And the Salvadoran officials, the Vice Ministers, General Zepeda and others, came and did a search of our office. But that didn't keep us out. We kept on working. They pretty much kept fooling us for the rest of that year. There was one requirement after another. We couldn't return unless we had purchased land. And there were a number of other kinds of requirements. We began to think, how much is it going to take to get us back, when they had tossed us out like we were human trash? That's why we took over the offices of the High Commission for Refugees. We held the office for two days, and then we took over the Salvadoran Embassy in Nicaragua for two weeks.

Next we had an appointment with the counsel, and we said that we want to go back, and he said, "No problem. I'll have an answer for you." And when he didn't have an answer, we came back and got all our stuff and we moved in there. We brought our cooking equipment and our pots and pans into the courtyard, and we washed and we set a little latrine in the corner, and we just lived there. We said, "We won't take it anymore." And after we set up the latrines in the corner, we did theater about the history of our community. We were clear. We would stay there in the Embassy until they gave us a favorable reply.

I think one factor that helped us was that the Salvadoran Embassy was right next to the Argentinean Embassy and the Columbian Embassy. The other ambassadors who lived in their embassies just couldn't sleep. We were making this noise. It was like we never slept. The ambassadors from the other two embassies would call the Salvadoran ambassador and say, "Can you get these people back to their country?"

We had set up deadline dates in January and February, but that never really happened. March 7th they sent a team to document us with our personal IDs and things. And that's when we left the offices of the embassy because they agreed we would be going back then. So on March 20, 1991, we boarded the planes to come back home. When we got to the terminal they wouldn't even let us go through the passenger terminal. They put us through the cargo terminal because they didn't want the Nicaraguan people to see us leaving.

The Christian-based communities met us at the airport. But the government put on their own kind of show about this. On the way back, as we were driving in, they put up a big banner which said "Welcome Salvadorans to Your Homeland." But behind the banner were five tanks and a squadron of troops. That was the reception we got from them.

> These are some reasons why we get these headaches about our government we have here, because of the way they tossed us out of here, and the way we were treated as we tried to come back to our country, and the way we were received.

With that said, Soledad turned to introduce Juan Flores, the man with the commandant's face on his shirt. "We'll ask Juan to tell us what happened once we got here."

"I would like to say that I want you to feel welcome," he said, "because your presence here motivates us as members of the community."

— 3 —

Juan Flores's Story

> It wasn't a very easy process, this whole repatriation. Part of the process of returning is having an idea of where you want to go back to. And we would ask the government if we could be located on these lands down here on the coast, exactly where we are now. That was rejected by the government.
>
> So we rented eighty acres of land in southern Usulután. But these lands were very unproductive, arid lands. These were lands which did not allow for any kind of development for the future. We were really worried. We were back and we just didn't see any possibilities, so we formed a commission to look over all the land to see what possibilities there were. And to look at other lands. But they just didn't see anything that looked appropriate. So the commission came to look at lands in this area.
>
> We were aware that refugees from Panama had regained this land here, and we talked to them, and they led us to those who headed up the cooperative. And they gave us the support to come back to these lands here.

So the commission went back to the people and talked about the land here, and how fertile it was, and we seemed to have the support of the cooperatives that held the land, and we explained to the rest of the community that we thought this was the best land for us.

I think it is very important for you to know how we make decisions. That is, before we make a decision, we have to bring it back to the entire community, for the community to decide. And by that means we make a decision or take an action. And that's how we began the movement of people into this area. It was a hidden movement. Three families at once, maybe four families at once. That's why it took nearly a month for the whole community to move over here.

When the first group came through the dirt road from the town of San Marcos Lempa, it was stopped and held by the military. The people were held right there in the middle of the road. They said to us, "There is no way we are going to let you pass, and we're going to get in touch with the United Nations, and you better go back where you came from." They accused us of a land takeover.

That wasn't true. We showed them the document we had from the cooperative that showed the legality of what we were doing, and the support we had to get these lands. But that didn't make any difference. The army told us, "You won't pass any further."

It was a time of anguish. We were in the hot sun on the road with children and babies, and we talked with the head of the command there, and the head officers back in the base, and it just was impossible. We told them, "We just can't take this anymore. We don't have any choice. We are going there, and if anything happens to us, you are responsible." The group was made up mostly of old people and women and children.

So we told the drivers we are going to drive right through the barricades. Me and two others, we started our trucks and started moving forward. The other drivers were not getting involved in this. Our two vehicles started to move, and the soldiers started throwing anything, big stones, anything, on the road to block our path. And as the soldiers were throwing the rocks, our people just picked them up and threw them back out again. We were a lot more than them, and any rock they could throw on there, we could remove four of them. It was really sort of funny.

The people cleared the road of the barricades, then they formed a human wall on either side of the road to let the vehicles pass through. They were in the road, and when the vehicle came to pass through, the people would open up and then close down again.

We got one vehicle through. Then the second one came and they shot the tires out. So we left that one there. So now we had to use some force to get through. And while all this was happening up at the main entrance at San Marcos Lempa, for four days we had people going in the back way through Tierra Blanca. That gives you some idea of how we got in, how we moved here.

Since we've been here, the government has come by and officials from the Institute of Agrarian Transformation. They said they were very worried about us, that they were concerned about our health, that the conditions were not very suitable back here, and they would really like to take us to better lands. But we said, "We don't want your support to move from here. All the communities around here support us, and we like it here. We are not moving from this place."

When they couldn't get us out of here by tricking us, they tried to persuade the people by sending the military, the army back here. So the military, who were initially bad, came here and this time they were very friendly, making friends with the young people, distributing candy to the children, and *piñatas*, and playing games. It was based on this scheme they had.

We said, "Okay, let's clarify this. If you want to help us, we'd like your help, but not in the way that you want to give it. If you really want to help us, then look at the problems that affect our community. The military won't let us leave. There's a roadblock right up here at the corner. Remove the roadblock if you want to do something to help us. They won't let food come into the community. So if you really want to help, get rid of that roadblock."

Also they wouldn't let construction materials pass through. Medicines. Anything for the community, they would hold up at the roadblock. "If you want to help us, don't bring back little candies and *piñatas*." So we asked them to leave and take their sweets with them, because their presence here threatened our security.

So they agreed to set up a meeting with the officials of the army. It was a pretty heated discussion. We were insisting that they leave, and they were insisting that they wanted to stay and live with us and be with us. And while we were talking, a lot of people from the community started to gather.

When all the community gathered, we asked them, "Should the military stay with us?" "No!" the people shouted. "The military should leave!" When they shouted that, all the soldiers hung their heads. So this was some of what happened.

The third thing they did when they weren't able to break our spirit with the military action was they brought in another group of people. You saw them there at the corner. The New Dawn. They are made up of paramilitary people, soldiers who have been recently released, ex-soldiers, and death squad people. The idea was for this other group to be in conflict or confrontation with us, which would enable them to set up a military base right where they needed it.

Then there was another community right next door to us. They said part of the agreements of the peace accords was that there wouldn't be these kinds of actions, and that we had to leave by February 1st. As proof of that, as they were standing there, there was a U.S. military adviser with them who was living in the middle of their community.

Ten times we walked down the road, and they stopped us, and asked us, "What is your name? Where are you going? What are you doing? What is your business?" Thanks to God, with the agreement signed between the government and the FMLN, things relaxed, and we have been able to travel the country much more freely.

This shows what they tried to do, to isolate our community. They denied permission of the international delegations to visit us, saying that they really needed a Military Safe Combat pass. We said, "That's not fair. These people entered the country legally, and have a right to go wherever they can, as long as they obey the law. So they have the right to come visit us."

This was just another form of breaking down the barriers. We had to meet with the head of the Sixth Brigade in Usulután and get him to sign an agreement that the internationals could come back and visit us. It has just been one incident after another here. It was an attempt to isolate us from everyone else. Even the United Nations High Command for Refugees, which was supposed to have some relationship with us because we are repatriated refugees, backed off and didn't do anything for us for a period of time.

But we feel good now. We have made a lot of progress, but it's been a tremendous struggle. People from other countries have been in solidarity with us, pressing to open up so many possibilities, and we've had a lot of help within the community. So we are grateful, not only for you, but for all the people on the outside who have worked to support us all this time.

"The government," added Soledad, "has not given us a nickel, not even a split nickel, to help with any of the construction or any of the other projects. The work we have done here is our own hard work, with international support to pay for the materials. We are just thankful for you because in some ways you represent that. No matter how many millions of dollars the government has received from your country and from other countries, it never goes to the poor. It goes to maybe their own people, but to the poor? No matter how much you gave, it wouldn't come back."

Then she added, "You might also be interested in knowing a little bit about how we organized, the projects that we have going on, and how we designed the work here."

"Why don't we save this for the morning," Sinclair said. "They talked about dinner at six. And it's past six. And we may need a few minutes to walk around and hang out. It's getting dark."

As the meeting broke up I overheard Bertsch talking to Sinclair.

"I wonder if you would ask Soledad something. When she was talking about the four nuns . . . " she began. She wanted to know if Soledad knew Ita Ford, one of the Maryknoll nuns raped and killed by the Salvadoran National Guardsmen on October 3, 1980.

Sinclair asked Soledad.

"She was with us," said Soledad. "She was one who meant a lot to us."

I caught up with Bertsch as she walked out of the pavilion. "Eilene, did you know any of the nuns?"

"Ita Ford was a college schoolmate," she said, her voice shaking. "I knew her and her brother."

Chapter Six

A *Cooperativa's* Ongoing Projects

In a nearby clearing, four wooden school desks and a couple of benches were scattered under a tree. Soledad stopped momentarily.
"This is our sixth grade," she announced.

Hiking up the dirt road leading through the center of the community, we arrived at the pavilion where supper would be served. A long wooden table was set with white plastic dishes, cups, and a pitcher of water, and several women were cooking over a clay fireplace. On a second fireplace a large black vat was filled with dough for tortillas. A door to the right led into a supply room, and from time to time several women peered out, curious about their visitors. Another table in front of the building held large basins for washing and rinsing dishes.

Since supper was not ready, several of us walked over to a field next to the pavilion to watch an all-girls softball game. About 12 to 15 years old, the girls laughed and shouted encouragement to their teammates, while onlookers behind the plate and along the third base line, yelled and cheered. It looked like any sandlot game back home, except for two differences. First, the batters. One after another, they stepped up to the plate, took a couple of practice swings, then when the pitcher threw the first pitch, rather than waiting to see if it was any good, they swung away, often connecting with the ball, then racing toward first base. The other difference? No boys played. They were either sequestered in the holding camps for the guerrillas, or in the army, or casualties of war.

At supper, our hosts served heaping platefuls of guacamole, beans, and fried *platános*. Then, eager to please, they ladled more food on our plates. I was stuffed. And in the back of my mind I could hear Torriera's warning not to waste any food. "The communities will be going without so we can eat," she had said.

"If anyone can't finish the food," Ventura announced, coming to the rescue, "give it to me."

Several people took up his offer and scraped their beans onto his plate. But instead, on impulse, I picked up a couple of beans in my fingers and fed them to a scrawny duck rummaging for scraps under the table. That was a mistake.

After we finished with the meal, we noticed a young girl, decked out in a white polka dot dress, white shoes, with white ribbons in her long brown hair, standing in the doorway to the supply room. It was her birthday.

That was all Gradie and Kempton needed to hear. Immediately they scrounged through their bags, producing a collection of worry dolls from Kempton and a box of crayons from Gradie. The child accepted the gifts, and stood wide-eyed and smiling from ear to ear as we sang "Happy Birthday."

With darkness falling, we stood in twos and threes under the shelter of the roof when Willison walked over to me.

"Ralph, let's talk," he said, leading me away from the others. "You really have to be careful with what you do. These people have no food. They are trying to give us what little they have, and it upsets them if you feed the ducks. I know you didn't mean anything by it, but the women are upset."

—— 2 ——

We left the pavilion and picked our way single file in the dark back toward the road that ran through the center of the community.

"I want to introduce you to the missionary nun responsible for working with the people from several surrounding communities," Sinclair said.

A bright moon threw our shadows on the ground as he stopped at a path that veered left through tall grass leading to a small, one-story building set back among trees. The house was dark.

"It looks like she's sleeping," he said. "But I think she would really like to meet the group, so we'll go in."

Sinclair went up to the front door and knocked. In the moonlight we could make out open windows, a front doorway, and a hammock and chairs on a porch. At first there was no answer. A few seconds later, a woman appeared in the doorway.

He hurriedly explained who we were and why we were there, and the nun, reassured we meant her no harm, told us that she served in the region as the link to religious services. "I'll be traveling to each of the communities tomorrow," she said.

"Is there a Mass here tomorrow?" someone asked.

"Yes," she said. "We'll be celebrating Mass for the community later in the afternoon."

Several people in our group said they hoped to be able to attend. Then, realizing we were keeping the good nun up, we wished her a goodnight and left.

"Sunday is a big day for her," Sinclair said, as we walked back to the road and started toward the bunkhouse where we had left our gear earlier. The night air was still unbearably hot and my pants and shirt were soaked with sweat.

"If anyone's interested," I said, "I'd like to try and cool off in the stream."

"If you go," Sinclair cautioned, "keep your head above water. And don't open your mouth."

Back in the bunkhouse the question foremost in everyone's mind was what the other accommodations looked like.

Reid sat down on the cot next to the door. "This is fine with me," he announced.

"I'll stay here too," I said.

Ventura said he'd join us, indicating he'd take the cot draped with the netting. I had packed netting that fit over the head from old camping trips, so I figured if the mosquitoes proved nasty, I'd survive.

"What about that swim?" I asked after the others left to scout out their sleeping arrangements.

Reid and Ventura agreed to give it a try, so we grabbed towels and flashlights, walked out the front door, and followed the path through the woods to the stream.

The water was warm and the bottom smooth underfoot, and in the center of the stream we squatted until the water reached our necks. That was when Sinclair's voice rang out.

"How's the water?"

Standing at the edge of the stream beside Sinclair were Willison, Sacco, and Romeo.

"Just what the doctor ordered!"

"What's the other sleeping quarters like?"

"You don't want to know."

— 3 —

Back in the bunkhouse, some workers snored and others talked in low voices. In our room, I eyed the gaps in the rough planking in the wall by my cot, pulled on socks, jeans, and a long-sleeved shirt, and lay on the cot. In minutes my dungarees and shirt were damp with sweat and before long I heard the high whine of mosquito wings.

Ventura was snoring, then the teacher from Barcelona we met earlier tip-toed in, prepared for bed, tossed and turned for a few minutes, and was quiet.

At that point a loud "thunk" sounded on the corrugated tin roof above my head. Then "thunks" came at different intervals, sometimes two and three together, slamming onto the roof, rolling off, and falling to the ground. Mangoes were dropping off the trees.

Later, while trying to avoid the mosquitoes and moving in and out of a light sleep, I was jolted awake by a raucous call, then a cacophony of roosters, squawking and cackling. Meantime, the workers began to wake up, talking and turning on radios to play music.

The next thing I knew Reid walked in the door.

"How's our group doing?" I asked.

"They are all up. They're washing by the well."

"How did they sleep?"

"What sleep?" he asked, laughing.

"What time is it?"

"Ten after six."

Outside the bunkhouse an early morning haze hung over the community, and up the road by the well two women pumped water into earthenware jugs. Then they placed the containers on their heads, and slowly walked off. At that point Willison came shuffling down a path toward the well.

"Where did you guys sleep?"

"We were squeezed into a one room shed. You wouldn't believe what we went through last night."

Bertsch limped by, her face ashen. "I have never experienced anything like last night in my entire life," she muttered.

Then I saw it. What came to be called, "The Hotel From Hell," a three-sided shack on a concrete slab, with black plastic walls, tin roof, wall-to-wall cots, and a hammock slung under the front overhang. McAllister, it turned out, had the good sense to commandeer the hammock, where he spent part of the night serenading the group with Scottish ballads then conversing with the roosters.

But the story everyone could not wait to tell was about this loud, incessant snoring coming from the back of the shed. Bertsch thought it was Sinclair.

"We couldn't believe he was sleeping so peacefully, and making all that noise. We were going to throw a shoe at him."

Finally, in desperation, someone did. But in the commotion that followed the loud snorting continued.

Then Sacco felt his cot shoved.

"I was about to tell off a roommate," he said, "when I realized it was a pig, grunting and pushing against the side of the shed."

All agreed, it had been a night to remember.

— 4 —

At breakfast Soledad proposed a tour of the community projects.

"I'd like to be able to check over your books," Ventura said, "so I can get a better idea of how the cooperative is running."

She agreed, so we left him in the community's office. In a nearby clearing, four wooden school desks and a couple of benches were scattered under a tree. Soledad stopped momentarily.

"This is our sixth grade," she announced.

A four foot square blackboard was perched against the tree's trunk.

"We don't have enough teachers, so the older students help with instruction."

As we continued through the community, half dressed children raced in front of us, crying out "*Norte Americanos!*" and men and women peered out of their shacks, the men pulling on shirts. We were a parade.

"We use every available space for gardening," Soledad said, pointing out small plots of corn and vegetables alongside the shacks.

Further up the dirt road we stopped under trees across from a large fenced-in field.

"This is the cattle project," she informed us, pointing to the area on the other side of a dry creek bed. To the left was a sizeable corn field, then a line of trees.

"The government will give the community fourteen head of cattle if we provide grazing and a source for water," she explained. "So we built the fencing," motioning to barbed wire stretched around the perimeter. "Then crews dug to find water."

Several sizeable craters marked the area where the men had dug with picks and shovels to locate water, but with no success. As a last resort, said Soledad, they turned to a padre in demand in Usulután for his dousing techniques. With that, she held her hands outstretched, demonstrating how the padre walked around the area with his divining apparatus, and when the end of the y-shaped twig dipped toward the ground, he told the men that was the place to dig.

"They found water fourteen feet below ground."

Next Soledad pointed to the corn field surrounded by branches piled at least six feet high.

"Why the branches?"

"The deer come to eat the young plants," she said, "so we cut down the branches as barriers."

"I have to get a better look at this," said Willison, jumping into the creek bed and scrambling up the other side.

Satisfied with what he saw, he walked back.

"Farmers had the same problem back home in Indiana," he said. "The deer and raccoons would eat the corn, so they devised a planting system that fooled the deer."

"How?" Soledad asked.

"The outer two to four rows of corn would be planted later and the animals would get to the unripe corn, and then they would lose interest in the rest of the crop. So they wouldn't touch the corn in the middle."

Soledad thought about that. "I'll tell the men what you said, and see if they think it would help."

— 5 —

At the top of the community to-do list, according to Soledad, was the construction of new ecology toilets invented in Scandinavia. The old toilets, simple framed structures with raised conical clay seats over holes, she said, allowed waste to leech into the ground.

"The water table under the ground is close to the surface."

A prototype toilet, a wood-frame structure on a concrete base, was set on an embankment about twenty-five yards behind a family shack. Inside were two holes, one capped with a wooden cover, the other with a portable clay commode that separated urine from feces. A pail of ash and lime, to turn the waste into fertilizer, sat on the floor.

Two concrete boxes behind the toilet held the waste. After a few months when one box filled, it would be sealed off and the clay commode moved over the other hole. By the time the second container filled, the waste in the first box was compost, ready to be added to the garden soil.

"This summer," she said, "the plan is for our construction crew to build ecology toilets for each of the community's seventy-eight families."

Next she led us to a working well, one of several projects repatriated families learned to build in Honduras. Two wheels were fastened to each end of a pipe shaft, with one end submerged in water underground. Plugs attached to a rope revolving around the wheels turned by a handle on top caught the water below, pulling it up to flow out a pipe into a concrete basin. Soledad demonstrated how it worked by turning the handle until water spurted out.

The following stop was at a squat structure in the center of a clearing. Roughly six feet high, with a shelf half way up the front, "*El Proyecto de Panadería*" resembled a small igloo.

"The older women of Nueva Esperanza asked for the oven to be built so they could bake bread for the community," explained Soledad. "They were feeling useless and left out of the cooperative's activities, and thought they could contribute to the community by setting up the bakery. Everyone supported the idea, the oven was built, and the women baked two days a week. Then the rainy season arrived and the women went on strike. They couldn't bake the bread in the rain, so the whole operation stopped."

The solution, she said, was to build a roof over the oven with space for tables and benches. "For about one thousand dollars, we could build the roof and pavilion, and the *panadería* would be operating again."

Earlier, Sinclair had praised Soledad as a shrewd community spokesperson with a knack for eliciting funds and materials from visiting delegations and international donors which, at the moment, was exactly what she was doing. She wasn't asking us to donate the money. But she was laying out the facts, talking about a specific need.

"Eilene," I whispered. "They need a thousand dollars. This could be a project for us. What do you think?"

"That's a great idea."

I walked over to Sinclair. "Do you think this would be a good project for us to get involved in? We could raise the money ourselves before we go home."

"What you do as a group is up to you," he said. "If you decide to do something like this, it will have to be a group decision. But empowering the people within an impoverished community is a good idea. The only thing I would be careful about is to make sure any monies donated to the community were stipulated for this project. You'd need to ask Soledad to draw up a contract."

"Would you ask her about this if the others agree to do it?"

"Sure," he said. "I'd be happy to help out any way I can."

"You think it is a good idea?"

"It's a great idea. Just be sure the rest of the group supports the idea before saying anything to Soledad."

Reid thought it sounded like a possibility. "But it would be up to the group. Maybe not all the people would want to donate money."

If each person donated $85, I figured we could make it happen.

Torriera was not convinced. "I still have to find my school for *La Hispanidad*," she said, "so I have to keep that in mind."

Ventura was checking books in the office, but the others tentatively went along with the idea, so Sinclair said he'd to talk to Soledad.

"You'll need a written proposal," he said. "I'll ask her to write one up."

He explained our offer and she went into the other room to consult information in a file cabinet. When she returned she said a proposal would be drafted and sent to the hotel before we left.

— 6 —

Heading toward the infirmary, we passed a little girl, no more than a year-and-a-half old, sitting in the dirt in front of a two-room shack, dressed in a soiled green T-shirt, her bare bottom on the ground, wearing a small beaded wristlet. Blotches covered her face. Her older sister, about eleven, walked out of the shack, picked her up, and was joined by her two brothers, one about eight and the other around four. Everyone pulled out cameras as the children posed together.

On the way to the infirmary Soledad mentioned the upcoming celebration at the cathedral plaza in San Salvador for the returning war-wounded convalescing in Cuba, the same event Mirna Anaya talked about the night we arrived.

"The people have been rehabilitated," Sinclair said. "They expect about two hundred and eighty will be returning to El Salvador. These are ex-combatants who lost arms and legs, or received other wounds during the fighting. Those who were able to use their hands have been trained to make prostheses."

"We plan to welcome about fifty of them to Nueva Esperanza with all their expertise," said Soledad. "One of the men lost his arms and legs in the war, and somebody had asked him what he could do. The man said, 'So, I still have my head. I can teach the people literacy.'"

Sinclair was hopeful we'd be able to attend the celebration.

Next on the tour was a coffee micro-factory. In a small shack an older man and a tiny bird-like woman ground corn into coffee with a series of machines driven by a gasoline engine. A blue fifty-gallon drum sat on a wooden platform by the rear wall with a pipe about eight feet long attached to the bottom. A foot from the other end was a joint with another pipe extending out about four feet to either side with spigots that fed corn into conical-shaped metal pails, then into grinding machines. The woman smiled and scooped up a handful of ground corn from a tray, letting the coffee dust slip through her fingers, proudly showing off the end product.

The community infirmary, run by a health promoter, turned out to be a three-room, cinder block structure. The middle room, a waiting area, included a bench and a rear wall partially stacked with medicines. An examination room with cots was to the left, and to the right was a small consultation room.

"Besides an infant mortality rate two to three times higher than other Central American countries, Salvadorans face three major health hurdles: malnutrition, respiratory illness, and diarrhea," the health provider said. "As an example of the outside aid we receive, look at all those bottles of Metamucil," she added, pointing to stacks of bottles against a wall. "We have no use for them. But that is what the international community sends us. And often when we do get drugs, they don't come with instructions telling us what the drugs should be used for."

Later, Barker wrote about the clinics we visited, saying they did not resemble anything she was familiar with:

> At one, as we toured, the leader was wiping away the dirt and grime from a table which held the bandages. There were no blood pressure cuffs, no thermometers, no exam tables, and certainly no EKG machines in sight. The clinics are run by women called "health promoters," who learned first aid, herbal medicine, and treatment of injuries in continuing education sessions, mostly as refugees in Nicaragua or Honduras. As I talked with these women, most of them less than twenty years of age, I reflected on their history. Community-based health care workers and clinics were the target of governmental repression during the war. Giving out advice, medications, and tender loving care was seen as subversive.[7]

— 7 —

By the time we left the infirmary, it was getting late. Folks had indicated the night before after speaking with the nun that they would like to attend Mass, but Sinclair reminded us we were behind schedule and would have to leave.

When I arrived back at the bunkhouse, Ventura and the teacher from Barcelona were standing face to face in the center of the room, embroiled in a heated discussion in Spanish.

"What's going on?" I asked Reid.

"I think they're arguing the relative merits of capitalism versus socialism."

Neither was backing down. Finally, Ventura turned away to pack his clothes. I should have given him time to calm down. Instead, I tried to explain the *panadería* project.

"Would you be willing to join with the others and donate money to support such a project?"

"No!" he answered abruptly. "I will not support such a project. I don't believe in handouts. These people need to become productive themselves. If, when they set up the bakery, we were to receive a 15 percent return on their profits, then maybe it would make sense. But the people need to be productive themselves."

For Ventura, versed in international business, the project was just another ill-conceived, liberal-minded handout.

"I am not so sure about this place," he added. "Did you see the houses of the community leaders?"

"No."

"You should see the house that Soledad lives in. It is quite respectable. They build concrete houses for the leadership, while the rest of the community lives in plastic huts."

He was upset. With the books, with the leadership's houses, with the teacher from Spain. To me, it made sense for the community leadership to build modest concrete houses. They hosted visiting internationals. The rest of the houses would be built in due time.

But checking over the cooperative's books had given Ventura a different perspective on Nueva Esperanza. "I don't agree with their procedures," he said finally.

Despite Ventura's reservations, Nueva Esperanza had been an eye opener. The *campesinos* refused to be cowed by government forces and, while laying the foundations for a community, were scraping out their daily sustenance from an unforgiving land.

Chapter Seven

Casa Clementina and Fr. Blanchard

"All across this country, in town after town, people are disappearing, and the army acts with impunity. They are in charge, fomenting fear and repression, and there is little that can be done about it."

After leaving Neuva Esperanza, our van broke down by the Rio Lempa bridge, which meant hitching a wild ride in the bed of a pickup truck to the airport to meet Tom Trebon, the last of our fellow travelers to join our group. By the time we arrived in mid-afternoon, his flight had landed hours earlier and he was not to be found, so we ended up hiring three cabs to ferry us back to the Alameda Hotel.

Later that evening the schedule called for dinner at Casa Clementina, the restaurant in San Salvador where we picked up Teresa the morning before, where we would meet with Dave Blanchard, the Carmelite priest and friend of Reid.

From the street, a little after seven o'clock, the restaurant was dark and appeared deserted, but inside several men sat at the bar with their backs to us. At the time, I felt uncomfortable, like we happened to be an unwelcome disruption. But it was all in my mind. Once we sat down and ordered drinks, then dined on the standard fare of *arroz con pollo*, I relaxed. Then Blanchard arrived.

The first time I heard Blanchard speak was at an organizational meeting at Sacred Heart University when all of us were trying to figure out whether the trip was feasible and who might participate. I had arrived late, and two men were sitting behind the front desk in the classroom. Minor Sinclair, a tall, dark-haired, fit-looking man, looked to be in his mid-30s. The other, heavyset and disheveled, and dressed in khaki pants, a peasant's shirt and sandals, slouched in the chair next to him. I thought he was a *campesino*, brought along to provide a native's view of his country.

But when it was his turn to speak, Fr. David Blanchard launched into a passionate, articulate overview of his pastoral work at Dolores Medina, a Christian-based cooperative for war refugees in the community of Calle Real outside the capital city of San Salvador. The man I thought was a *campesino* was a priest with a Ph.D. from the University of Chicago, an accomplished author, lecturer, and friend of Reid.

When he finished his presentation, I went up to ask his advice.

"I'm having serious reservations about this trip," I said. "I have little to offer these people who have gone through so much suffering and I don't even speak their language."

"That's exactly why you should go," he said. "The Salvadorans don't expect anything from people from the outside world. But at this critical time during the peace accords, an international presence is particularly important in El Salvador. It helps keep the army in check."

— 2 —

At Casa Clementina, with our chairs now set in a circle, Sinclair said, "Lets reflect about what has happened so far. It's good to share ideas, and then we'll hear from Dave about his work at Calle Real."

We talked about Tierra Blanca, Hacienda California, and Nueva Esperanza, and what we thought of their chances for success. Then the *panadaría* project was mentioned. To my surprise, several people said they felt coerced into agreeing to donate money.

"What choice did we have?" Willison asked. "How could I have refused when you asked me with Soledad standing in front of me?"

I had no idea that people felt that way. Donating funds for a roof so the older women could bake bread in inclement weather seemed a no-brainer.

Then others joined Willison.

"We would have preferred to think about it," they said.

"This needs to be talked about at another time when we meet as a group," Sinclair said. "Let's table this topic until the meeting of the last night when everyone has had the chance to reflect on the entire El Salvador experience."

— 3 —

"Casa Clementina is part of forty cooperatives," Blanchard began. "All the profits of this place go to the cooperatives. And especially to support the work of women. We provide work for women of the cooperatives, especially Hacienda California and Nueva Esperanza. This place has been open for three months, and it has been very successful. In fact, we have been full almost every night."

"Maybe you could fill us in on what is happening in the country now," said Sinclair.

"El Salvador is a fascist state," Blanchard said. "The oligarchy controls everything. The government, the law, the military, and the flow of money."

To make his point, he recounted the story of Nelson Molina Ayala, a young artisan in the carpentry shop at Dolores Medina. "When Nelson was about eight he lost his mother. The army stopped them one day, cut off the mother's lips, raped her repeatedly, then ran bayonets through her body. Cutting off the lips of the women, was a way of terrorizing the people so they would not collaborate with the popular organizations or the FMLN. The mother and son were in the wrong place at the wrong time."

Traumatized, the young boy fled into the mountains, and eventually found his way to Calle Reale several years later. By then, said Blanchard, something miraculous had happened. In his head, perhaps as a way of dealing with the trauma of his mother's rape and murder, he had created a series of paintings, over 200 of them, which he could describe in detail.

Nicknamed "Gazoo" – "the little runt" – after a character in *The Flintstones*, Nelson suffered from poor eyesight, so Blanchard managed to buy him glasses. Then with his sight restored, and relying on the visions in his head, the young man started painting on wooden crosses and knick-knacks in the carpentry shop, surprising everyone with his artistry.

One day, Blanchard said, Nelson was walking on a dirt road in the cooperative with his girlfriend when he was stopped by four ex-army men demanding his shoes.

"This could happen anywhere," he said. "All around the world, people demand shoes, money, or a jacket. It happens in East L.A. and it happens in Bridgeport."

Next they pointed to his glasses. "They were aviator-style prescription glasses costing six hundred colones," Blanchard said. "When he refused to take them off, one thug stabbed Nelson, killing him instantly."

Blanchard paused.

"And now we are talking about justice in El Salvador!" he said.

He repeatedly went to the National Police who told him no arrests could be made unless they had orders or a witness. And when Blanchard obtained a judge's order and returned to the police to demand the arrest of the men, he was told to forget it because they didn't pick them up in twenty-four hours.

"I know all four of the men," he said. "And even though I continued to press for their arrest, they went free. The boy was an artist. The glasses reinforced his belief in himself. So he refused to give them up, and he was killed. And the man who killed Gazoo had killed two people before. All of this suggests where the peace accords have left this country. The reality is that nothing has changed. All across this country, in town after town, people are disappearing, and the army acts with impunity. They are in charge, fomenting fear and repression, and there is little that can be done about it."

— 4 —

The Gazoo murder, a nightmare of a story, dug its way into our psyches, prompting me later to write the following prose poem.

A Plea For Justice in El Salvador

We heard your story from a Padre you must have loved.
He told us how you lost your mother that day
In the mountains. He said you were only eight years old,
And when the men in uniforms grabbed your mother,
Throwing her to the ground to rape her, you ran terrified,
The screams of your mother ringing in your ears.
But you must have turned momentarily, when the soldier
With the dreaded Atlacatl insignia on his arm,
Ripped your mother's lips from her face with his knife.

I can understand how that moment, and what happened
Directly after, when the men plunged their bayonets
Into your prostrate mother . . . once . . . twice . . .
three times . . .

Ten times . . . yes, a full twenty-seven times, traumatized you,
Left you without eyes with which to see . . . for years.
I wonder how you knew it was twenty-seven times?
I think it would be important for you to know that,
But how did it happen? Did you creep back
Through the thickets of brush and trees in the darkness
When the army men were off to some new diversion,
To kneel over the lifeless body of your mother,
And count the wounds?

So it is easy to understand how, growing up a refugee
In a strange land, you moved into a separate world of visions –
Of radiant, clear, strong colors, placed ever so carefully
Here and there on those canvases in your mind.

A full two hundred, your Padre said. And every one complete.
He said you could call up each and every painting,
Recounting the contents to your startled listeners.
So I understand. I know how coping with death
  takes many forms.
But to create two hundred paintings in your head!

II

But this is not your whole story. This is only the part
That tells us who you were when you arrived at the *carpintería.*
For years, the world had grown dim to your eyes,
And only in the confines of your mind could you see
The lines so deeply etched, the reds, yellows,
Greens and blues, juxtaposed just so.
Your Padre told us when they realized you couldn't see,
They went ahead and ordered glasses, in an aviator style.
I wonder what you must have thought when you placed those
Miraculous lenses on that first time? We know what happened.
Padre told us how you took up brush, letting the deep colors
Drain from your mind over the surfaces of those cards,
And boxes, and crosses. Explosions of color and design,
Your talent astonishing the good Padre of the *cooperativa.*

So when you were holding the hand of your girlfriend,
And you met those four ex-army thugs at dusk on
  that dirt road,
I think perhaps you must have wondered if your mind
Was playing tricks on you. It must have thrown you
Back momentarily to an earlier, darker time,
That lay hidden beneath all those canvases,
Back to that fatal mountain scene of years ago.

"I want your shoes," one said, and so, unwillingly,
you gave then up, not wishing to create a scene.
Another said, "I want those glasses," pointing to the Padre's gift.

You must have known who he was, must have shuddered
At the terrible knowledge of his reputation among your people.
And you, thinking to yourself, no . . . these glasses are my life.
So you said, "no," surrounded by the four ex-combatants,
Your girlfriend's eyes darkening with fright.
But what could you have been thinking when you said "no"?
What moved you to stand and face your tormentors?
Was it the spirit of Romero? Of Ellecuria and Segundo Montes?
Was it the spirit of all the war-wounded, saying in solidarity,
"No!"
And how did it feel when that cold steel entered your stomach,
Just before it slashed upward through your heart?
You must have felt the sharp steel plunge through
The thin wall of muscle, just before your eyes
Rolled upward, never to see again, the blood curling
Past your teeth as you crumbled toward the ground.

III

"This is what happens in El Salvador," the good Padre said,
his eyes scanning our group. "Yes, this is the reality of
the peace accords." And the Padre's story is not over yet.
Only the part about the boy's death.
But perhaps, gentle reader, you do not want to hear
About the Padre's frantic attempts to see justice done.
"There's a killer free in our midst," he said. "And we have
No idea who he will kill next. We only know
He's killed before, and surely, he will kill again."

And what to make of the remarks of the *policía?*
"Padre, you have no witnesses," they said. Repeatedly,
to the Padre's pleas for justice, he was told,
"It didn't happen. You have no proof."
No . . . no proof. Only the body of a poor
Salvadoran artist from your *carpintería,*
And the colors that spun from his visionary brushes.

— 5 —

"You have to realize," Blanchard said, "the peace accords brought great happiness to the people of El Salvador. There was such a feeling of exhilaration. They rang the church bell continuously. People were laughing and crying in joy. A new dawn was about to be created in El Salvador. But now, months later," he cautioned, "the reality has set in. We are living in extremely dangerous times. This period right now is more dangerous than any other time in recent memory. There is the illusion of well-being in the land, but the reality can be found in the story of the young artist from my church. That's how the army operates. The National Police get their orders from the military. They are in control of the country, and the result is the people have no recourse."

As far as Blanchard was concerned, by June of 1992 the integration of the police agencies and the guerrilla insurgents into a new policing and control apparatus had not adhered to the stipulations of the accords.

"The three police agencies have taken new names, are still together, maintain the same strength, and live in the same barracks," he said.

With Blanchard and Reid deep in conversation, I slipped out of Casa Clementina and walked across the road to Blanchard's pick-up. He had said he would give us a ride back to the hotel, and while I stood in the dark by his truck, I couldn't get the Gazoo story out of my mind.

Moments later, Reid joined me. "It sounds worse than ever now," he said.

"That was some story."

"Maria Teresa was talking before. She heard a report on the radio that three people had just disappeared."

"It seems Blanchard has come out in the open over this case about the boy," I said. "He could be targeted by the death squads."

I was reminded of a story Blanchard told during one of his campus visits in the spring about a visiting priest from Europe working at Dolores Medina. The priest had asked Blanchard's permission to attend a peace rally in San Salvador before the signing of the accords. He said he thought about it, then told the priest it was too risky. The army had spies. They took pictures at peace rallies, marking people for retribution. A priest at the rally could be traced. The cooperative could suffer severe consequences.

But now, with the killing of the *carpentería* apprentice and with the promise of the accords in question, it seemed Blanchard had left caution behind and was speaking out openly against the army and the justice system.

Standing with Reid by the vehicle, waiting to be ferried back to the hotel, I got myself in such a state that I wasn't sure it was safe to ride with Blanchard. But at that moment, he appeared, jumped into the truck, turned on the ignition, and started wrestling with the gear shift.

"This truck is badly in need of repairs," he sighed, grinding into reverse. "But it's not a priority at this time."

— 6 —

Back the Alameda, Sacco was talking about what happened when the rest of the group left the restaurant.

"When we were getting into the cabs, three teenagers came up to us and started speaking rapid Spanish," he said. "I couldn't understand what they were saying."

"They were asking directions," McAllister said.

"This was very odd," said Sacco. "Natives asking *gringos* about whereabouts. I had to usher Louise into the vehicles, since she seemed to think it was just quaint and they were being conversational."

Sacco was sure the boys were assessing the possibility of pulling off a robbery.

In the hotel lounge, Blanchard was holding court surrounded by our group, talking about a start-up factory which he hoped would be fully operational in two years. Run entirely by the women in his cooperative, the plan was to produce hospital smocks and apparel on a profit margin with dividends going to workers based on productivity.

"Fifty percent of the profits would be applied to factory expansion," he said. "I'm looking for worldwide distribution to provide economic stability for the people."

But, like the situation at the La California salt works, the project faced problems.

"Wealthy people control much of what happens economically in the country," he said, "and they are not happy with any sort of competition. In fact, one contractor who monopolizes parts of the industry is very difficult to do business with."

Then Blanchard talked about a project somewhere out in the country, hampered with graft and corruption siphoning off international funds.

"It's a ditch digging effort," he said, "and tons of money have been allocated for the project. But nothing is happening. The project exists on paper, and the money is disappearing. I knew a member of the State Department, and I told him I would take him to look at the project. The U.S. official said that wasn't necessary. Also it wasn't allowed because of where the project was taking place. But I persisted, and so we drove out to the site. Nothing was there. The official couldn't believe what he saw."

This fascinated Ventura, who barraged Blanchard with questions. But it was getting late, it had been a long day, I was tired, and when the comments started running into one another and I had no idea what they were talking about, it was time to bail out.

Chapter Eight

A Ravaged UES Campus

"The real proof and validity of our work was that we had thousands of students thrown into jail. As of this morning, we still have 21 of our students in jail. We have had rectors killed. The rector of 1980 was assassinated."

The story of the University of El Salvador [UES] at the time of our visit was one of struggle: to stay afloat financially despite 30,000 enrolled students, to rebuild a campus infrastructure decimated by war and the 1986 earthquake, and to reclaim its intellectual place in the hierarchy of Central American institutions of higher learning.

Viewed by many as a breeding ground for FMLN sympathizers and combatants, and dismissed by its detractors as a "flop house for *campesinos*," the institution, known also as the National University, had more than earned its reputation as "the university that refused to die."

"In the 1970s the University of El Salvador was the most prestigious public institution in the region," Sinclair told us as we walked through the rubble-strewn campus. "It had the best library, top academic personnel, and a quality graduate school program. Now the university is in a desperate struggle against the enemies of progress and education who have tried to destroy it. In the past fifteen years the university has been occupied by the Salvadoran military four times, one rector was machine-gunned to death, the entire administration rounded up and jailed, and the university itself forced into exile."

Evidence of the war and the earthquake was everywhere. Barbed wire was strung along pathways, bullet holes pock-marked the exterior walls of buildings, and in one instance the Chemistry building – once an imposing four-story structure – was reduced to a concrete framework surrounded by piles of bricks.

"Military governments ruled El Salvador from 1944 until recently," said Sinclair as we made our way to the Administration Building for a visit with the Rector, Fabio Castillo. "As El Salvador's guerrilla insurgency gained ground against the government during the 1980s, the university community has been repressed. People have been killed for carrying a student I.D. and professors have been 'disappeared' for writing articles against the regime. For months at a time, a military cordon encircled the campus and everyone who entered and left was searched for subversive materials. The best profs are no longer here because of finances. They can't afford to work here."

In other words, a once-proud institution of higher learning was staggering against formidable odds. But not without hope. Fabio Castillo, known in El Salvador as "the Grandfather of Education" – a man, Sinclair informed us, highly respected by all factions of the university – was doing his utmost to restore the school to its former academic standing. At one point, Sinclair said, five people were in the running for the position of Rector, but when Castillo, serving as Rector for a university in Costa Rica, declared his candidacy, all of the others, out of respect, pulled out of the race.

"Currently, the Vice Rector, Catalina Machuca, a very capable woman of *campesino* background, basically runs the university," he told us. "Castillo, because of his experience and high profile, has assumed a role similar to college presidents in the U.S. He attends meetings, gives lectures, solicits support, and generally shoulders the responsibility of bringing the school back to its former prestige. He's a very active, enthusiastic man. And his conception of academic excellence differs from that of others."

"There are those who believe," Castillo had said, "that the goal of education for the masses is to train poor people for menial labor and to train a few others to supervise. We believe differently. All people should be taught to use their reasoning, to think critically, to build a society in which they believe. That's our purpose here."

— 2 —

In a spacious room that once served as a cafeteria and was now partitioned into office spaces by filing cabinets and desks, we stood around waiting for our interview with the rector. Signs on the desks announced "*Fiscal General,*" "*Secretaria General,*" "*Secretaria de Plantification,*" "*Generencio,*" and "*Vice Rectoria.*" Castillo, it was explained to us, had been called off campus and instead we would be meeting today with the Vice Rector.

In her office, Catalina Machuca, a short, stocky woman with curly red hair and dark-rimmed glasses, and dressed in a black shirt and white skirt, sat in a high-backed leather chair behind a large, arc-shaped wooden desk that held a vase of fresh flowers and piles of stacked papers and reports.

"Good morning to everyone here," she said, motioning us to sit on the couch and chairs in a semi-circle in front of her. "I apologize for the wait to see you. This meeting was on the Rector's schedule in the office, but it wasn't on his private schedule, so he apologizes to you. He has an event in Santa Ana, so he has other commitments today. He can't see you this morning, but you could meet with Dr. Castillo at another time."

After introductory formalities, the Vice Rector launched into an overview of the current state of the university.

Testimony of Catalina Rodriguez M. de Merino

At this point, we are the only public university. This university is 151 years old, the oldest in Central America with the exception of the Universities of Guatemala and Nicaragua. There has been a tremendous religious influence within our university, but since the movement for independence, the university has declared itself a secular institution and began a relationship with the state. The university is open to everyone without discrimination of faith, sex, race, or political opinion.

I think that probably the most important thing about this university is that it has adjusted itself to this moment in the history of El Salvador. Maybe that's the reason we've had our difficulties with different administrations of government. We have been a university of critical thought, accompanying the great majority of those people who have been dispossessed, and many of our alumni have been fighting for the revolution and the people.

Since the peace accords, the university has changed with a new vision academically, a new vision of reconciliation. Right now we are very involved in curricular change. Traditionally, we had eight different departments with three different branch universities, one in Santa Ana, one in San Miguel, and one in San Vincente. The three branch universities have been transformed into universities that are multi-disciplined within themselves and that can respond to the needs of those local areas. The curricular change we are involved in is based primarily on the belief that education should serve the greatest needs of the people.

If we are really to lend the resources we have here at the university for the benefit of the people, we would have to disperse our students and faculty throughout the country for more in-depth research. And that takes place through the Social Projection, our national outreach program.

Through the Office of Social Projection the university comes into contact with the different communities and the people of the country. Students and teachers go out into the countryside and undertake their research, return to the university, process that information, then they return and address some of the specific needs of that community. The methodology is highly participatory. For example, the people of our country have been fooled and tricked so many times in the past that they don't believe anything. So our program helps them to trust their own intuition.

You may wonder how does a university go about doing this? We have gone to look for support from the greater international community. Throughout the years of the war, the university received tremendous help from sister universities, different associations, and non-governmental institutions which have tried to enable us to continue to progress during these very difficult times. We have support from the European community, from Germany, the Netherlands, Holland, from exchange universities, and from other organizations which help countries in the Third World. Based on that help, we survived as a university, and in some ways we fulfilled our mission.

We also have relationships in North America with several universities, and most recently the agreement with DePaul University. And most of the Mexican universities. We are members of the regional federation of Central American Universities, but we have very little relationship with universities in South America.

Also we work closely with the Lutheran Church, the Episcopal Church, the Baptist Church, as well as the Catholic Church. They have always been very helpful to us. We have a very close relationship with the University of Central America [UCA] and the Lutheran University here. When the situation allows for it, we cooperate with the private universities, and there's somewhere between thirty to forty of them in El Salvador. You know, we're such a big country! We can afford many private universities! The only problem is these private schools have no students because the people can't afford to pay the tuition. This gives you some idea of the kind of relationships we maintain.

In times of curricular change, our university is very much on the cutting edge. We are responding to the needs of the people. Our biggest problem? Human resources and the quality of our teachers. Another issue for us is the introduction of new books and materials that respond to the present moment and are not obsolete. Then we have real problems with our library and library system. We don't have the trained staff to manage. It needs to be revamped completely. Also we need computers, vehicles, etc. In addition, our financial resources for faculty salaries are very inadequate. For the budget at the university, public funding from the government has not been increased in twelve years despite the fact that our whole student body has changed and practically doubled.

During the war years, the number of students actually declined a little bit. During the war years we had four thousand, six thousand, maybe eight thousand entering students. But since the peace, we've had twelve thousand students enter this year. Which shows you the needs of growth. We need equipment, space, resources. We really can't prioritize our needs because we really need everything. For example, where we are sitting here now is not an adequate space. This building was the cafeteria for the university before the earthquake in '86. In the earthquake of 1986, 70 percent of the buildings were condemned. Not even with the National Reconstruction Plan has the government included any resources for the rebuilding of the National University. And it's not because we haven't made any efforts. We have met with many representatives from the government to ask for our inclusion in the National Reconstruction Plan. They have been given four hundred million dollars to rebuild after the war, and none of that has been directed toward the National University.

So we see our mission as the better training of university faculty. We have fifteen hundred professors here, based on three general levels of teachers. But our best professors left because of the war, and secondly because of the freeze on salaries for the past twelve years. The average professor here earns between two hundred and fifty and three hundred dollars a month. The Rector earns four hundred dollars a month. Few people have even a Master's Degree. The only departments that have doctorates would be the faculty of medicine and dentistry. All the others have left.

The real proof and validity of our work was that we had thousands of students thrown into jail. As of this morning, we still have twenty-one of our students in jail. We have had rectors killed. The rector of 1980 was assassinated. In 1981 the entire Deans' Council was put in jail. The library, the art collection, and the fossil collection were bombed and destroyed. While military personnel surrounded the university grounds we continued our programs. The university gave attention to the earthquake victims. We continued the services of health care, dental care, and psychological health in all the marginalized communities in the city and in the outer communities. Now we are even at greater strength.

For example, the university has assumed responsibility for programs for the education as well as the healthcare of all the ex-combatants, and this is healthcare in its integrated form. The director of the United Nations agency has signed an agreement with the National University for the university to receive eight hundred and seventy thousand dollars. But the Minister of Planning, as well as the Minister of Education, opposed that and they are doing everything they can to boycott our programs. So we have to work without any outside funding, and not a penny from the government.

The government says we don't have the skills to be able to provide the programs with any continuity. The Minister of Education said the university doesn't have the strength. We have agreed to a meeting with the Minister of Education, but so far that meeting has not been confirmed. Right now, the government is in an adversarial relationship with the university because of our identification with the needs of the majority of the people. And they're scared that we will mount an excellent program in education as well as in healthcare.

One of the curricular changes being introduced is starting with the Social Projection Program at an earlier stage when the students come here. In the first stage, the students go out to the community, and they can see the real needs that the people have. And that can help focus their studies at the university.

Before the peace accords, we were stopped and asked for identification at the roadblocks. Now there is free access to any community you want to go to. But there are still some hard-headed military people who don't want us to have access to the people.

In conclusion, we need to raise the academic training of faculty in general, helping them develop their research methods, and we also need to improve incentives for people so that they don't leave the university in a year or two.

After the meeting she led us outside behind the Administration Building for a group picture, then explained that an intern from her office would accompany us on a tour of the campus.

While we assembled for the photo, I couldn't help thinking that this woman, a shrewd administrator, must have been wondering how our small New England Catholic university could possibly be of assistance to her institution now close to destitution. And at the same time, in the back of all our minds was the charge given to us by our own president to attempt to lay the groundwork for a plan of cooperation with a Salvadoran university.

As it turned out, after returning to our campus, and following a series of communications, a collaborative agreement was drawn up and signed by the presidents of both institutions which in time translated into two delegations of faculty from UES participating in a U.S. Agency for International Development [USAID] training program hosted on the Sacred Heart campus. But the possibility of setting up a program of ongoing faculty and student exchanges between the two universities never materialized.

— 3 —

It was after eleven o'clock by the time we started the campus tour. Our first stop was the art department where a student show hung on the walls, then we walked past a building with a large banner hanging from the third floor with the words *La Construcion de la Sociedad Salvadorana* [The Construction of the Salvadoran Society]. The two top floors had been ripped apart by either shelling or more probably the earthquake.

Everywhere on campus, large murals, painted in bold colors, covered the sides of walls, shouting out slogans or depicting Goya-like images of whitened bodies, fires, darkened figures executing people with machine guns, and always the white doves hovering over the scene. In front of one building, Sinclair pointed out a statue riddled with bullet holes in the head.

"A reminder," he said, "of the government's military offensive on this campus, and of the university's resolve to honor and memorialize its stance for freedom during the Civil War."

In an open-air canteen across from the university library, casually dressed students sat at tables shaded by trees, talking, reading, and eating hot dogs, tortillas, and drinking sodas. The scene could have been taking place on any campus in the world. Yet, a few years back, this was a campus under siege.

At a nearby table a male student and his coed friend were hunched over a paper, checking what turned out to be a prof's handwritten notes.

"Do you mind if I look at your paper?" I asked. "This is what I do in the States. I'm a writing teacher."

They understood, and the young man handed over the paper. In the margins I read several neatly written comments in English.

"You have a good instructor," I said, handing the paper back. "He's asking you to add more examples. It will make your paper better."

The student nodded, and I left the two of them bent over the paper again.

Over the entrance to the building next on our tour a sign read *"Cuando el justicio el dercho entran el conflicto sera siempre la justica"* ["When justice and right enter into conflict, justice will always prevail"]. Students, on break between classes, lounged in a large lecture hall on rows of wooden seats angling down to a center stage. The walls were covered with murals, a red FMLN banner hung from the ceiling over the stage, and behind the stage was a large painting of two figures surrounded by names of the fallen. To the left was a 10 foot square mural of Herbert Anaya Sanabria, the husband of Mirna, and next to him a painting of a young boy, hands clasped in prayer. Other murals portrayed Romero, Dr. Ernesto Guevara Serna, Che Guevara, and the sprawled figures of the slain Jesuits with the words of Ignacio Ellecuria, *"El problema radical de los derechos humanos es el de la lucha de la vida en contra de la muerte"* ["The fundamental problem of human rights is the struggle between life and death"].

Later, we visited the university media center, where an instructor explained about the journalism, photography, and TV programs, and an impressive list of lower-level and advanced courses. The student enrollment topped five hundred, the instructor said.

The student newspaper, *Primera Plana* [Front Page], turned out to be an eight-page paper produced by the Journalism Department, concentrating almost exclusively on current issues. Only one feature article in the May 27 issue, a story on a band, was devoted to a topic other than the political scene, and even in that story the lead singer Felipe was quoted as saying his band focused on issues of the war and its aftermath.

Meanwhile the instructor mentioned the years of video footage shot during the war. "We need someone with technical expertise to help us make sense of all the footage we have."

"Maybe Becky Abbott would be interested in doing something like that," said Spence.

Abbott was an experimental filmmaker in our media department. Partly in response to the faculty exchange idea outlined later in the two universities' collaborative agreement, and because they could fill a specific need, Abbott and Spence traveled back to El Salvador in the spring of 1993 to assist with the project.

Before leaving the campus, we assembled in a group to take a picture in front of a huge wall mural titled, "*Depués de 500 años la Resistencia Continúa*" ["After 500 Years of Continued Resistance"]. To the left of the mural were the words:

Estas son las voces
del silencio que rompen cadenas!
Voces que surgen de la muerte.
! para dar vida!
Voces lentas, calladas,
que transportan la verdad.
Palabras libertarias! No Gritadas!
sino, dichas quedamente,
con voces de razón, amor y revolución.

[These are the voices of silence that break chains!
Voices that rise out of death to give life!
Silent voices that carry the truth.
Liberating words! Not shouted,
but spoken quietly, with voices of reason, love,
and revolution.]

— 4 —

Accompanied by an administrator of the National University, we stopped for lunch at a buffet-style restaurant in the city, then drove out to visit two communities where UES students donated hours of required community service. The Social Projection program that required community service for graduation intrigued us. It worked here, it seemed, but would it be feasible back home? El Salvador had just gone through a war, and the need for involving students in service projects was acute. It was true that back home parts of Bridgeport looked like a Third World country, and issues of poverty, homelessness, and unequal educational opportunities called out for action, and our school had from its beginnings stressed volunteer efforts on the part of our students. But "requiring" service was something we had to think about.

"How often have our students been asked to make personal sacrifices for the betterment of the community or a particular individual?" asked Willison.

Not enough, we agreed.

"How many hours of community involvement do our students participate in without expecting money or personal recognition?"

Good question.

"What examples do our adults and institutions set?"

Again, the answer was not impressive.

Before we left to visit the first project, Torriera came up with an idea. After listening to the Vice Rector explain the extraordinary needs of the UES, she stayed behind to meet with Dr. Rolando Labrador, the head of the English Department. On our campus we were building a new state of the art language lab. So why, she asked, couldn't we donate the old lab, still in good working condition, to the National University? After seeking Trebon's input, Torriera made the offer which was promptly accepted. The details of packing the lab and sending the boxes to UES would be worked out over the summer.

The first stop for the afternoon was a dental and health clinic in the colony of Los Olivos, a community of 30,000 people crammed into eighteen hundred cinderblock row houses built on the side of a hill across the Rio Acelhuate in the Northwest outskirts of San Salvador. We arrived to find houses facing one another across narrow walkways and toddlers peering at us shyly from behind their mothers' skirts.

"One young boy in particular caught my eye," Trebon said later. "He was ten, I would guess, with a most striking and beautiful face. He sat on his haunches and watched us, moving away only when one of the group wanted to take his picture. He held a tin can wrapped in string with a kite attached. I had seen kites up against the hillside, and here was one of the flyers."

The facility, a one-story clinic staffed mostly by women, was run by a doctor, a heavyset man in a hospital coat, who ushered us into the dental care area, a well-lighted, spacious room where patients in green hospital gowns lay on raised cushioned platforms next to trays of dental instruments. Two-person teams of technicians wearing plastic gloves and surgical masks worked on the patients, talking in muted voices, their instruments clicking against teeth.

In an adjacent room, the diagnosis area, we met the chief health care provider, a male nurse, who talked about his upward battle with communicable diseases. "As you would expect," he said, "there is a high incidence of disease in the community."

Backed by the National University, the medical center served as a functioning healthcare facility, modest in scope when viewed against the overwhelming needs of the residents of Los Olivos, but vastly superior to anything we saw at Nueva Esperanza or Sister Elena's.

Outside the clinic we came upon a class of youngsters under the watchful eyes of older children and their teacher. Books and papers lay scattered over desks as they wrote vowels on their pads, then pronounced them out loud.

Kempton immediately fell into her role as teacher.

"Say your vowels," she said.

"A, E, I, O, U!" the children shouted back, happy to show off their learning.

The next community consisted of rows of one-story cinderblock houses sprawled over the foothills of a mountain. Built by the government after the 1986 earthquake, this was home, we were told, for war refugees, ex-combatants, as well as a number of death squad members.

"Students come here to canvas the population," our UES guide explained. "They fill out questionnaires, trying to assess the needs of the people, then they return to the university where they collate the information and then decide what actions to take."

But problems had surfaced.

"The activities of the death squads are a cause for great concern," she said. "There are instances of killings. And many ex-military personnel, traumatized by the war, are not receiving the services they need."

As we piled out of our parked van, a dozen youngsters clambered up a small hill next to the sidewalk and sat watching us. In a nearby field we saw a large blue and orange canvas tent with a sign *Circo Barnun Bross.* Small flags attached to ropes from the top of the tent hung listlessly in the afternoon sun.

Two young girls stood on the wooden ramp that led to an arched doorway into the tent. Behind the girls, panels announced the main attractions: "El Ninja," a black garbed figure; "He Man," decked out in red knee-high boots, yellow trunks, and straps crossing his muscular chest; "Skeletor" in a blue body suit, with a dark blue hood and cape; and "Coco Rico," an "*El Especial de Poison*" in a yellow coat covered with red and green patches. Off to the right, a trailer sported a large clown face and two ticket windows. The girls on the wooden ramp threw up their arms as if celebrating the arrival of the circus. Meanwhile, near us on the hill by the sidewalk, several older boys joined the youngsters.

"There's a large mix of people thrown together here," the guide said. "There's been several murders. We tell our students to be on guard when visiting the area. Too many people are living in a confined place, with some of them enemies from the war."

With that reminder of where we were, we walked up the road for a closer look at the village. Row upon row of one-story concrete buildings, each with a door and one window, faced across narrow walkways that dipped in the center forming latrines. Electrical wires ran from a pole to several buildings and occasionally a TV antenna sprouted on a roof.

At one point two children ran toward us, and one of them, a little boy not more than four years old, dressed in a T-shirt and shorts, wrapped his arms around Gradie. His little sister in a blue jumper, her ponytail held by a red tie, stood next to him waiting her turn. Gradie hugged the small boy, then motioned to the sister to join them, which she did, smiling from ear to ear.

As we walked back toward the van, a raggedly dressed fellow in his twenties started talking to Ventura. Suddenly the young man began shouting and waving his arms. Dressed in business suit and tie, Ventura tried to remain calm, and continued walking toward the van, the young man trailing alongside.

"I don't like the looks of this," Sacco commented. "See that other guy," he added, pointing toward another fellow standing nearby. "This could be a ploy. I don't trust the way that guy looks. He is in cahoots with the guy talking to Jose. We should get out of here before something happens."

The wild-eyed fellow continued to shout at Ventura as they approached the van, becoming more and more agitated. Ventura quickly crossed the road and boarded the van.

"That could have been a set-up there," Sacco said to him as he sat down. "I didn't like the looks of those guys."

"He wasn't making a lot of sense," Ventura said.

"What was he shouting about?"

"He kept yelling, 'Why don't you get out of here. You don't belong here.'"

— 6 —

Driving back toward San Salvador to drop off our UES guide, we thought about the Social Projection Program and how it was working in settlements on the outskirts of the city. It made perfect sense, filling a specific need, and the students, committed to the cause because of the fervor for social action on campus, were performing a useful service while at the same time gaining a feeling of accomplishment, a real sense of partnering in the effort to mend the ravaged Salvadoran world.

The question remained: could such a program requiring community service work on our campus? The need was there. Our city newspaper was full of stories about the open warfare fueled by the drug culture between rival gangs on the streets of Bridgeport. In the early '90s entire sections of the city were fire zones, with residents afraid to leave the protection of their residences after dark.

The result was that people from the surrounding suburbs refused to enter the city.

But what could we or our students do? At the moment, this was a question without an answer.

As we approached closer to the city, tin-roofed shacks and hard scrabble farms morphed into produce stands and shops. On the concrete steps in front of one store a man lay sprawled on his back.

"Did you see that?" I asked Reid.

"Yes."

"That looked like blood on his chest."

"It did."

McAllister had just finished relating a story he heard earlier that morning from a UES instructor. A couple had been found tied to a pole at an intersection in the center of the city. Both were nude and decapitated. The head of the woman was placed in the crotch of the man with his penis in her mouth.

I looked at Reid. "Maybe that wasn't blood we saw, and the man was just drunk."

"For his sake, I hope so."

Chapter Nine

The Hierarchy and Romero's Chapel

"Peace and social justice are very important. And the relationship between the two has much to do with our chances for peace. The lack of these two things caused much of our problem."

The following morning, June 16, the schedule called for a 9 A.M. audience with Arturo Rivera y Damas, the ninth Bishop and the fifth Archbishop of El Salvador, named to the position after the 1980 assassination of Oscar Romero.

"When Romero's predecessor died," said Sinclair, referring to Archbishop Chavez, "the choice for bishop was between Damas and Romero. At the time, it was thought that Romero was much more conservative and Damas much more liberal. But the two men worked closely together. After Romero's death, Damas was the most important influence to bring together the opposition. He's thoughtful, deliberate, and he's excited about his relationship to SHU."

The relationship Sinclair referred to had started when our university conferred an honorary doctorate on Damas on May 17, 1990 for his work with the poor. At the same time it was hoped that the conferral of the degree would send a message of solidarity to the people of El Salvador following the assassination of the Jesuits at the UCA in 1989.

In the Archbishop's offices, we were ushered into a room with a large conference table. Damas, a short, trim, fit-looking man in his late 60s, dressed in gray slacks, a white shirt with clerical collar, and a dark gray jacket, walked in and stood at the head of the table, a welcoming smile on his face.

"Your Excellency," Trebon began, "we are very pleased to be here. The President of our university, Dr. Anthony Cernera, has asked me to give you this letter with greetings from him."

Damas took the letter and sat down, folded his hands on his lap, and looked directly at each of us as we introduced ourselves.

"We have come here to find out what has happened in the last few months," said Sinclair. "We know you have had a large part in the activities of recent times."

"We are very pleased to be able to receive you," he said. Then he turned to Sinclair. "Maybe it would be better if we translated," he added, indicating a preference to speak in Spanish.

With that, Sinclair filled him in on our visits to Tierra Blanca, Nueva Esperanza, and the National University, then mentioned our scheduled visit the next day to Calle Real, the community where Fr. Dave Blanchard worked.

"David Blanchard, who is in the parish, has done much writing about the situation in this country," Damas said, "and it seems he has much material to publish some books."

Interview with Damas

> I think there are two aspects to consider in El Salvador. Peace and social justice are very important. And the relationship between the two has much to do with our chances for peace. The lack of these two things caused much of our problem. And the doctrines of the National Security and the Marxist and Leninist responses of the FMLN have created much of our problems.
>
> We are trying to implement the peace accords, which end on the 31st of October. Two bodies have been charged with the supervision of the accords, and there is good will, but there are concerns about the delays.
>
> The other area which needs much attention is the area of human and spiritual values. Our crisis came from a lack

of values, where a party tried to impose its values on an entire country. International pressure, facilitated by the signing of the agreements, pressure that must be continually brought to bear on these people, will give both sides the political will to achieve peace.

Q) What can Sacred Heart University do?

A) To help our situation, I think it would be best if you worked through an institution here, another university, and worked for peace. Then you could work together for a lasting reform. That is what occurs to me at this time.

Q) Your excellency, which university would be willing to help us?

A) The university with the most prestige is UCA, the Jesuit University. Also Einstein University and the Technical Universities. Also the bishops have a university in Santa Ana. However, size is not important.

Q) I wonder if you could talk about the National University and the fact that they are working with people in the country.

A) The National University [UES], is the largest. They probably have thirty-five thousand students, and we have a friendly relationship with them. I didn't mention them because of the politicization on the side of the left. There are efforts to correct this problem, but we are too early in the process to judge their efforts.

Q) Could you define the term "*mystica*" for us?

A) There is a great sense of religiosity among the people. They practice many devotions. The Vatican II Council has tried to enrich our religion even through the years of the conflict. The people are very persistent. They will not allow themselves to be beaten down. The Christian-based communities that started ten years ago were very politicized. They fed into the armed resistance. One was aligned to the ERP, the Revolutionary People's Army, and the other to the FPL, this was the popular church. But these were more the exception than the rule.

The other component is that they have served to contain the growth of fundamentalist sects.

Q) What are the rich doing to help the peace process?

A) Communities of faith take place in the parishes of the wealthy, but not with the same vitality. The Churches have approved that the accords be followed, and we are trying to see that this happens. We also try to promote the encyclicals. Last year we held a week long conference on *Rerum Novarum*. Also there is social doctrine given each week at the end of the homily, and this is roundly rejected by the wealthy.

The former administration of government, the Christian Democrats, implemented many structural reforms. The present government had done away with many of these reforms. But the peace agreements have supported those reforms, especially with land distribution. The land should be passed over to the people where the FMLN are. In these places, there is very strong discussion about redistribution measures where the owners are selling to the people. The people are trying to buy the land.

There will be better distribution of the land, but not everything relies on land. But it is an important part of the problem. It is very important that the land reform be peaceful. So there is pressure on those who don't rely on the land to sell it to the people who subsist on the land. And this gives me hope for the future of our country.

Education is something very dear to all of us here. We see that the richness of life is the person. The person's development is an integral process of body and soul. And education is the way to develop the people. The war has been expensive in costs to health and the education of the people. Just this last week the teachers' union is on strike, which I believe is an injustice because it tramples on the rights of the students to learn.

Q) Are you still perceived as a liberal leader in the church for the cause of peace?

A) In El Salvador, the archbishop has been close to the people. Monsegnor Gonsalves, Monsegnor Romero and I have tried to continue this closeness to the people based on the Christian idea that the person is created in the image of Christ, and the people confide in their pastors.

— 2 —

The session over, we thanked Damas, and walked down the hall to meet with Rafeal Uriotia, the heavy-set, garrulous Chancellor of the Archdiocese and Director of the Social Secretariat, who spoke about the church's efforts during and after the war, and its roles in the evolving national dialogue.

Rafeal Uriotia's Talk

I give courses, and I work in a parish in the afternoons and evenings. I'm also entrusted with the cause of the canonization of Monsegnor Romero. And occasionally I go to the beach . . . when I sleep.

In the area of social work, we have four or five things going on at the same time. There is much work to be done for the people. The General Secretariat has about eighty-five people. Our current projects include leadership, administration, a program for permanent housing (rebuilding after the earthquake), health promotion, program and project design, and educational work in the communities.

Our fundamental work is based on humanitarian assistance: health, housing, food and nutrition, and basic utensils. Basically it involves people going back to their homes after the war, the repatriated people. We have programs for health and permanent housing, programs of agriculture for self-subsistence, programs for the promotion of women, and a school for appropriate technology. We also support the housing and food needs of FMLN combatants in their areas, along with the support of CARITAS [Catholic Relief Services]. And then there is what the Archbishop has asked me to do. So this is how eighty-five people keep busy. In all of this we are looking to train our staff here and in other countries.

Through the twelve years of the war we have not accepted any money for humanitarian assistance because it was not appropriate to accept money from a country that was also supporting the war. The U.S. government has supported a political regime. But the exploitation of the poor has been alarming, and there is a cry for social reform. For example, the government in power can't impose a tax on rich companies for a source of income for the government. Couldn't tax them in any way. So they have a graduated sales tax, and the harm falls on the poor people.

After the Jesuits were killed, we refused to accept any money which at its root made us silent or that would not allow us to look for justice. The gospel values are not to be negotiated, not with sister Church. Not by the government nor by any amount of money. Now we are open to talk about other services. But often our values and principles are not respected. Even the Catholic Relief Services adopted a stance that was pro government, and we did not accept their intent. The money is good, but we cannot allow the hurt of our people.

Here are two examples. Catholic Relief Services placed certain restrictions on their credit loan programs. We base credit at ten point two percent. They wanted fifteen point five percent. And each community would need a letter from the mayor. I was responsible to see that the letters were signed by all the mayors. Then they wanted to have the names of all the people who would be the beneficiaries. But that is very dangerous. Even in this moment of peace, we know that people are being pulled from their houses and being killed. So these are some of the problems stipulated by AID [Agency for International Development]. The Church has a history of helping people and we are proud of that. We want any aid that comes to respect our perspective, and to respect the people and not abuse them.

Anything that you can do for the National University means a great deal. The Catholic University has other ways to help. But the National University is much more in need of help.

In the office on the wall is a map which shows the settlements where the FMLN are located. We wanted to see how the settlements were divided up in the diocese. Because of the history of the Church, it never assumed its historical role. In 1981 the archbishop created the Social Secretariat. I'm the second. The first was forced to leave the country in 1989. The Salvadoran branch of CARITAS never looked to the problems of the war. So Romero founded this Social Secretariat which now attends to all the victims of the country.

We are a channeling agency for so many things. We were seen in a bad light by the government and half of the bishops. We are looked upon as Communists, as friends of the FMLN and dangerous people. In January the European community looked to us to provide for the needs of the FMLN. In January Damas was named President of the Bishops Board. Based on that we sent a proposal to CARITAS to work in the camps. We did not want to take on this work unless CARITAS also did. And if this work is considered Communistic, then let's get the whole Church involved.

For women, we have productive programs, programs that would help to raise their spirit in the face of the *machismo* of the Salvadoran people. But mostly our work is with the widowed women, to get them productive work.

Since the signing of the accords, the violations of human rights have decreased tremendously. There have been cases, but most are viewed as isolated cases. In a situation of so much military structure, it is difficult for the military to even control itself. At the mid-level commands, they can take actions. But I think little by little, we are learning what it means to live in a democracy. It means not just to vote. And this is thanks to all the social structures and to the war, unfortunately.

For us, the government economic policies are seen as an exploitation of the poor. People in government would refer to it as the gains brought about by neo-liberalism. For the people in power, the policies of neo-liberalism have brought the goods. Even during the war, production increased, and people got more money. Even now when President Cristiani comes to power. But it has helped only a few, especially the rich.

In our history the Salvadoran people are idiosyncratically capitalistic. We are naturally pushed toward private property. We are a business people one hundred percent. If you lose your job, the next day you are out driving cars. Salvadorans don't die of hunger. They work, or they organize to make war. We are looking for a system that is capitalistic, but that respects the rights of the workers, not only those of the owners. If in El Salvador we don't create the basis for social justice in the next twenty years, then there will be another war.

On the causes of the war, clearly the land ownership is one of the principle causes. But also the exploitation of the *campesinos* is the other. And the *campesinos* made the war.

The Chancellor's wide-ranging talk, emphasizing the initiatives of the Church for the poor in the postwar era, reinforced much of what we had already seen and read about. Admitting that not everyone in the hierarchy was "on board" with the message, nevertheless the Church was attempting to walk in the shoes of the people, championing economic and spiritual welfare, and positioning itself at the forefront of the drive for justice.

For lunch we ate at a courtyard restaurant in the heart of San Salvador, across the street from a building painted white with a sign announcing "*Academy Sagrado Corazon*" [Sacred Heart Academy].

Instantly, the cameras popped out, with members of our group intent on capturing a photo of our namesake institution, complete with razor wire strung across the roof of the building. A circular to the right of the Academy's front door listed the subjects: "*Corte y Confeccion,*" "*Bordardo a Maquina,*" and "*Capacitation en Macquinas Industriales*" [preparatory courses in sewing and industrial machines].

"Not exactly our curriculum back on campus," someone observed. Inside several girls sat in front of sewing machines stitching pieces of cloth, training to become seamstresses, hoping for a sought-after position in a maquina factory – notorious for long hours, poor wages, and lack of workers' rights.

"These trade-oriented academies offer their students a better chance to support themselves," said Sinclair. "But the salaries provide little more than a subsistence living."

— 3 —

Driving to the Chapel of the Divine Providence, where Archbishop Romero was assassinated on March 24, 1980, we passed through an affluent section of the city with manicured lawns and tropical trees surrounding gated mansions with high cement walls topped with razor wire, guarded by armed uniformed personnel.

Up a long drive the meticulously groomed grounds of the chapel and cancer hospital were bathed in sunlight. As we left the van and made our way toward the chapel, we couldn't help but recognize the reverential atmosphere about the place where only a dozen years ago the unspeakable had occurred.

"The man who did it was a dentist in town," Sinclair said. "He was hired, probably by the military."

Many people, he explained, including diplomats in El Salvador, believed that Roberto d'Aubuisson, a right-wing radical and former National Guard officer and one-time national intelligence chief who studied in the U.S. at the International Police Academy in Washington, ordered the assassination. Dismissed from the military in October of 1979, and arrested in 1980 after an unsuccessful coup attempt, he returned to found the ARENA party in 1981.

"Romero's assassin was known as a marksman," Sinclair added, "and he never admitted to who had paid him. Romero had just made his famous homily asking the military to stop killing their brothers and sisters."

In a pew halfway down the center aisle, I stared at the sanctuary blanketed with fresh flowers, and the plaque marking where Romero had fallen, and felt I had come face to face with the nexus of good and evil – where the life of a revered prince of the church ended with the crack of an assassin's rifle.

"I want to tell you that Romero had a profound effect on me," McAllister wrote later as he wrestled with his visit to the chapel. "I still don't know what happened in the chapel, but Romero has changed my life."

As we filed out of the chapel, Sinclair stopped to talk to a nun. "Would it be possible for us to visit Romero's house?" he asked.

"This is not a usual time for visitors," she said.

He explained about our delegation and our purpose for visiting El Salvador, and the nun agreed that "an exception would be made."

She led us from the chapel to a modest cottage behind a low stone wall with a small front garden, a grotto with a statue of the Blessed Virgin, and a white pedestal supporting a bronze bust of Romero.

Inside was a micro-museum. Pictures hung on the walls of the front room, and the vestments Romero wore when he was shot were displayed in a glass case. His blood had turned dark with age.

When the nun escorted us to Romero's tiny bedroom with its simple cot and writing table, it became clear that, as much as was possible in his daily life, this man of God had moved away from the trappings of his ecclesiastical office to live in monastic simplicity.

CHAPTER TEN

THE AMERICAN EMBASSY

"About the death squads, I don't know. A special investigative agent was shot two days ago. Usually it's a question of being in the wrong place at the wrong time. We did reach a very discouraging phase between March and May."

Later in the afternoon we visited the newly-constructed, multi-million dollar United States Embassy in the district of Nueva San Salvador. The juxtaposition of the simplicity of Romero's living quarters against the ostentatious display of American bigness at the Embassy, a fortress of buildings surrounded by walls and checkpoints dominating the countryside, was jarring and embarrassing.

Around 3 P.M. our driver made a U-turn, and stopped in front of the main gate.

"You will have to turn in your passports when we go upstairs for our meeting," Sinclair said. "It's a formality. You'll get them back when we leave."

At the first security checkpoint in an out-building, a guard asked us to leave cameras, bags, and "anything that could be used as a potential weapon." Then we were led into the main building and a spacious lobby housing two bullet-proof glass enclosures – one with a clerk who took our passports and asked what our business was, the other with a Marine guard standing at attention.

"I don't like the looks of this place," said Kempton.

"What's the matter?" I asked.

"They are going to hear from me about this place. It's too posh!"

"It really does have a fortress-like look. It's in bad taste," added Spence. "Anyone who took Art 101 would know that."

"Do you mind if I ask you why you are here?" the Marine asked.

"We're here to study the country after the peace accords," I said. "From a university in Connecticut."

I got the feeling he suspected we were a bunch of liberal Communist sympathizers.

"I'm deliberately not combing my hair and putting on lipstick," said Kempton, miffed.

At that point a woman in a purple dress with a name tag identifying her as Pamela Cory Archer, Director of the USIA [U.S. Information Agency], greeted us, ushered us through a thick metal door with several locking mechanisms, then led us upstairs to the third floor into a cavernous conference room, and invited us to take a seat at a round table, large enough to accommodate half the Notre Dame football team.

"It's very King Arthurian in here," Archer said, looking around.

The walls were covered with fabric and the table was at least fifteen feet across and twice as long.

"Until '78 we were strictly TV and radio," she said. "Then in '78 we took over the educational and cultural aspects of the Department of State."

Archer explained she had been stationed in El Salvador for the last two years, was about to return home, and then before leaving us introduced a blonde woman in a gray suit.

"This is Barbara Stevenson," she said. "Barbara will bring you up to date and answer any questions."

— 2 —

"I've been covering politics here for the last couple of years," Stevenson began. "Now I'm covering the peace accords, and it's been an almost perfect cease-fire. There have been no shots fired in anger since the signing of the accords. And no fighting since then.

So we see no reason to go back to war. The accords have been stunningly successful."

Successful? After witnessing the breakdown of the accord stipulations with the presence and testimony of Apolo at Hacienda California? After Fr. Blanchard telling us the present moment in El Salvador was more dangerous than any time in recent memory?

"Maybe you have questions that I can help answer," she said.

"What about the status of the National Civil Police Program?" Sacco asked.

"It requires a lot of administrative work," she said, "but we're making progress and we're hoping the academy will open by July 25. In the first two classes, there were seventeen hundred hopeful participants."

She explained that the testing was ongoing, and included one class per month. Participants had to pass a physical that included sit-ups and pull-ups and a medical exam, then they took written tests to determine their aptitude for the curriculum. Also they were subject to psychological testing, and finally an investigation of the background of the applicant.

"Would the new Civil Police be open to former members of the FMLN?"

"The tests did not specifically bar ex-combatants."

"What about the recent activities of the death squads?"

"The number of incidents is down. But the follow-up is very poor. The judicial system in this country remains very weak. About the death squads, I don't know. A special investigative agent was shot two days ago. Usually it's a question of being in the wrong place at the wrong time. We did reach a very discouraging phase between March and May. Nothing was happening. The government was not doing its job in overseeing the disbanding of forces. The police were not being demobilized, and the land reform was not being initiated. But on May 11, the FMLN and President Cristiani got together and agreed on some guidelines. Last Friday a recalenderization plan was drawn up, and beginning June 25 the FMLN will hand in 25 percent of their weapons."

Problems, she said, were compounded by the fact the FMLN wanted the old security forces dissolved, and the compliance on the part of the government didn't really happen. The Treasury Police were scheduled to demobilize over a period of twenty-one months to approximately two thousand personnel. And, if the laws were passed, the FMLN agreed they would demobilize by at least 80 percent. The National Police, numbering about eight thousand, would remain in the urban areas, while the National Guard would stay in the country. "Basically checking driving licenses and registrations," she said.

It sounded like the security forces, rather than making substantive changes, were simply switching names, and I got lost trying to keep the different units (National Police, Treasury Police, National Guard, Military Police, Hacienda Police, Civil Police) straight. Maybe, I told myself, Sacco could make sense of it all later.

— 3 —

Ventura wanted to know about the economic reforms.

"The treaties call for a gathering of business, labor, and government to talk about economic programs," she said. "Some of the FMLN leaders want sweeping socio-economic reforms."

She pointed to the current growth in the economy, but said the '94 elections would be important. The deregulations were good, she added, because they dropped tariffs. But there was some question about the trickle-down effect of the money.

"In '94 the peace issue will be behind us," she said, summing up, "and the issues will be more economic."

At that point Trebon asked about on-going educational programs.

"The country hosts thirty-eight universities, but thirty of them are principally trade and vocational schools," she said.

"What about the withholding of funds from the National University that had been set up by UNESCO [UN Educational, Scientific and Cultural Organization]?" Sinclair asked.

"There are problems holding up the disbursement of funds," Stevenson agreed. "It's because of the perceived politicization within the National University. There are reports of the FMLN occupying a floor of the library. There are tremendously dedicated people who are paid very little who work there, but the university can't survive on monies given from the government."

"What about the issue of land reform?"

"The biggest estates have been broken up – over eleven thousand acres," she said. "But in the mid 80s the implementation of the two hundred forty hectare limitation on land holdings took effect. The FMLN wanted lands that exceeded twenty-four hundred acres to be broken up. So there was some violent kicking of people off their lands. The FMLN took over roughly a third of the country, and now there are many property issues that must be settled by COPAZ [National Commission for the Consolidation of Peace]. With recalenderization in effect," she said, "the future looks promising. Both sides do not want to return to war."

Listening to her talk, it seemed two different narratives of the post-war realities were emerging. So we looked forward to our visit to Fr. Blanchard's community the next day, thinking the testimonies we would hear there might clarify the issues. For the moment, trying to piece together the situation on the ground depended in part on who you were talking to, and their political affiliations and agenda.

In closing, Stevenson admitted the judicial system was not working.

— 4 —

The meeting ended around 4:30, and we walked downstairs to the office where we left our passports for security purposes. It was closed for the day. So much for coordination among Embassy offices. Willison, Spence, and Gradie agreed to stay to retrieve the documents as soon as embassy personnel could locate them. Then we discovered we could not exit the building before problems with our names and IDs were ironed out.

By the time we passed through the outer gates, we breathed a collective sigh of relief. The Embassy complex was stuffy and oppressive, and its footprint a slap in the face of impoverished Salvadorans. Later, we learned they looked upon the Embassy as one more instance of American stupidity and greed.

On the way back to the hotel, we stopped at the National University where Trebon, Bertsch, Torriera, McAllister, and Sinclair were to meet with Fabio Castillo around 5 P.M. This was to make up for the missed meeting the previous day. Later I was told the meeting was cordial, and included discussing a proposal for a cooperative agreement between the two universities that included collaboration in teaching and research as well as faculty and student exchanges.

That evening we arrived at a *papuseria*, and were joined by Chester Wickwire, invited by Sinclair to dine with us. A graduate of Yale Divinity School who had served as university chaplain at Johns Hopkins, he had worked in Baltimore with black urban youth, the Black Panthers, and migrant workers, and was highly respected in Central America because of his efforts since 1979 with the poor in Nicaragua, Guatemala, and El Salvador.

"He championed the cause of teachers incarcerated during the early years of the war in El Salvador," said Sinclair.

It turned out that the reason why he joined us, besides Sinclair wanting us to meet him, was to set up a plan for him to hitch a ride with us to Perquín, the rebel stronghold in the mountainous northeastern province of Morazán close to the Honduran border, the last community we would visit in El Salvador.

"It will take about five hours of driving time to reach Perquín," Sinclair said. "But it's an important place. The territory wasn't generally accessible during the hostilities."

Largely held in rebel hands, the area had witnessed some of the war's most brutal fighting.

"The area is not considered safe," he cautioned, saying heightened security measures would be necessary. "You'll need to stay together, and be more aware of your surroundings."

— 5 —

Later in our room, I asked Sacco if he could explain what he had learned so far about the different police organizations.

"Before the peace accords," he said, "several forces were responsible for maintaining order: the Military, the National Police, the National Guard, and the Treasury or Hacienda Police. The National Police controlled the country, similar to our own FBI. The National Guard operated as more localized police and were directed to disband by the accords. The Treasury Police, charged with supervising farms, also were directed to cut back on manpower. Before the accords, the Treasury Police and National Guard numbered about ten thousand combined, but now they were to demobilize to about two thousand. The National Police were supposed to stay at the same level, but since the accords they swelled their ranks from fifty-nine hundred to eight thousand, adding men from the demobilized other forces."

The police and military forces were "works in progress," he said.

CHAPTER ELEVEN

CARLOTA AND DEEMA

"When they heard the army was coming, they ran into the mountains to hide. But some of the women had very small children, and they couldn't hide very well. So the army found them, and over there where they found them, they killed them."

By 7:30 Wednesday morning we left the hotel for the drive to Dolores Medina roughly nine kilometers north of the outskirts of San Salvador, a community of about forty families in the larger, repopulated community of Calle Real.

"To the west of Calle Real looms the volcano of San Salvador," Reid wrote later in the *Sacred Heart University Review*, "and to the northeast, in the distance, rises the volcano of Guazapa. On the weekday morning we traveled to Calle Real the highway, broken by long stretches of gravel and dirt roadway, was choked with traffic of cars, trucks, overcrowded buses, and pedestrians, most traveling south into the capital city."[8]

Of the twenty-five thousand people residing in the several smaller communities of Calle Real, most, we were told, were either ex-combatants or *campesinos* displaced by the war. Established in 1986, Dolores Medina was the base of operations for Fr. Dave Blanchard, where he had devoted himself to setting up a faith-based community with self-sustaining micro-businesses.

— 2 —

"One of the children, a girl if eleven or twelve, met our van and welcomed us," Trebon said. "She had been waiting. She grasped hold of my hand and said, '*Hola! Buenos Dias.*' As we walked on to the village she held my arm as if to lead me to the house where our breakfast was to be served."

Blanchard, dressed in a long-sleeved white cotton T-shirt, khaki shorts, and sneakers, greeted us then asked us to follow him down a cement walkway bordered by one-story brick houses, each with a large planter in front filled with bushes and flowers. A woman and two children waited for us at the far end of the walkway.

"You are the breakfast guests of Carlota and her family this morning," Blanchard announced, introducing the woman, and leading us into her house past a room to the right and a kitchen to a small enclosed courtyard in the back. A six foot wall of concrete bricks stood to the left with a planter filled with flowers and vegetables. Red flowers decorated the other walls and burlap bags, shirts, and blouses hung on a clothesline. In a rear corner was the *baño.*

A pudgy two year old, decked out for the occasion in a flowered shirt, red shorts, and sneakers, sat in a child's chair staring wide-eyed at us.

"That's Kevin," Blanchard said.

Kempton, taken with the young boy, motioned with her hands for him to come to her. His sister picked him up handed him over.

"Oh, Kevin," she gushed, hefting him in her arms, "you are substantial!"

At that point, Blanchard introduced Rick Jones, a man in his mid-twenties with curly blond hair and a handsome Nordic face.

"Rick coordinated the first part of the DePaul trip the summer before," he said, explaining that Rick decided to stay at Dolores Medina to help run the community enterprises.

We all sat around the oilcloth covered table while Blanchard, coffee cup in hand, began the conversation by talking about the community bakery.

"They make some incredible pastries," he beamed.

"How many people work there?" Willison asked.

"Three or four. They make twenty-five kinds of bread, rolls, and pastries. And recently they started making croissants. Now they are working to get a mixer."

In spite of the progress in the community, many items were still missing at Calle Real, Blanchard said. "We collect donations back in the States, but we need somebody to drive down with them."

"Get a truck," Willison said. "I'll drive down in August. Then I'll go back in September."

"How long does it take?" someone asked.

"I've done it in six days," said Blanchard. "I think it's about four thousand miles."

"That's nothing," said Willison. "I've done thirty days in a row."

After listening about his worldwide treks, I had no doubt: if he said he could do it, he could.

The women served heaping platefuls of corn tortillas made from corn mush baked in corn leaves, fried *platinos*, rolls from the pastry shop, and coffee. It was a feast. And while we ate we peppered Blanchard with questions. Kempton wanted to know the percentage of women in the National Police.

"There's a battalion of women in the National Police," he answered. "They are prepared for times of emergency."

"What about birth issues?"

"She is 'giving light now' is how Salvadoran women describe it," he said. "Roughly 50 percent of the babies are born at home with the assistance of a mid-wife. We have three here, but it is not a profession. They just do it. The government has a certification program for mid-wives, but the people just do it themselves. It has to do with personality. This person is my friend, is closer to me."

"Do they use medicines?"

"They use chocolate to stimulate milk," Blanchard said, "but people die in childbirth."

Then talk turned to the cooperative's residents, where they came from, the effect of the war on their lives, and how the Dolores Medina cooperative started.

— 3 —

"Carlota, the woman of this house, was a rescuer in the mountains," Blanchard said. "These women founded a refugee camp at Calle Real. They grew in strong leadership, and they got more land, some illegally, some at the tail-end of the land reform. This place was originally a garbage dump. It was bought from the Church. They took out a loan, built houses, moved into their homes, and one month later an earthquake destroyed everything they had built."

"The people living here now come from the early revolutionary movement, from popular organizations, and from organizations within the Church. All revolutionary organizations go through crises and reforms. It is a delicate thing to ask the people about. But this is not a handout community. These people built this place by hand, they took out loans, and they will pay those loans back."

"I need to check on the status of the rest of the day's meetings," Sinclair said, standing up and excusing himself. "If I don't make it back by tomorrow . . ." he laughed, his voice trailing off.

"Earlier in the morning a woman was taken to the hospital with cholera," Blanchard said, changing the conversation. "I want you to understand that she didn't get it here. She works in the market. Which means that you should know that you don't eat anything from the market." Then he said, "I took shots for cholera, and I got cholera."

"Yes," Barker interjected. "The shots are only supposed to be about fifty percent effective."

At that point, yesterday's Embassy visit came up.

"Just look at the place," said Gradie. "It is an imperialistic structure. It looks like a plantation house, a fortress."

"I've got a story about that place," Blanchard said. "The FMLN commander, Joachín Villalobos, was given a tour of the U.S. Embassy and shown the extensive security measures. One member of the party said he thought the Embassy compound was 'a monument to U.S. genius.' Villalobos responded, 'Actually, it is a monument to your stupidity.'"

"One of the big fallacies in this country," said Blanchard, "is to train people to go out on their own. The result is they leave the worker cooperatives. Here we train people to better the community instead of themselves. These people spent four or five years in refugee camps, and then they came here and worked for two years to create this place. You need to create the structure to allow people to work in the community. Otherwise it is like peeing in a river."

He continued, "In this country, only big businesses can import. So we need to buy from our competitors. In other words, they have a preferred status. Supposedly, the peace accords have opened the importation business. Sure they have. They are supposed to have disbanded the National and Hacienda Police, as well."

Ventura was speaking to the side with one of the women. "They got up at five o'clock to start our breakfast," he announced, impressed.

"Your hosts wouldn't have it any other way," Blanchard said. "They take pride in serving the *Norte Americano* guests in their homes."

With breakfast over, we sat on chairs and benches along the side walls of the small courtyard, and pulled out notepads and tape recorders. Then an anthropologist we had met at the National University joined us, her small child in tow. She was studying the Salvadoran people for a degree at Chapel Hill.

"I told them that you are going to be visiting the community today," Blanchard said, "and that it might be helpful if they could develop a context for you to see where they came from. I also explained that I would explain to you that they are a little embarrassed to do this. They don't think of themselves as special people, and they don't understand why anyone would want to hear their stories."

Carlota, her dark hair pulled tightly into a pony tail, spoke first. She avoided eye contact and looked up at the sky, her voice rising and falling.

— 4 —

Carlota's Story

We'll talk a little bit about how we began to organize and to work in the struggle, from the place where we were. The first struggle to organize involved a meeting with a priest whose name was David. We said during these meetings that

> in order to struggle to better ourselves we first of all needed to organize because the way that we lived was so terribly poor. We had to struggle to overcome great slavery, the slavery under which we lived. There were few who had much. And there were most of those who had nothing. There were days we had very little to eat, and there were days when we had nothing to eat.

"Let me translate," Torriera said. "This is an extremely moving story. She's explaining her life little by little, in pieces. It's a continuation from her memory, things from the past. She is saying that they realized they had to organize, and she is talking about 'they,' 'they,' 'they,' and it's confusing what she means by 'they.' But she says that they knew it was time to start a unified organizing to confront 'they.' They all had children, and the children had no time to be educated. And everyone had very little. They had the minimum of food. And then they realized that that was not enough, and that they could be organized. So all the children left, and they were not here any more. But they had nothing. So they had to bring them the things that they needed. So the women . . ."

"She is saying they incorporated into the army of the struggle," Blanchard explained. "It's a euphemism for saying her two boys entered the armed struggle as guerrillas."

"That I understood," said Torriera. "But it is very interesting the way she is presenting it, closing the eyes and bringing it back. It is extremely moving."

> We organized ourselves in the houses in order to provide them with food and other means of sustaining themselves. And "they," being now the powerful, said that what we had set out to do was destroy the country.
>
> The army said that they had to be destroyed, those who had fled to the mountains, because they were bad, and they were going to destroy the country. So the army came and they started to hunt the people who were in the mountains. And in the houses were many women and

children, and in the beginning at night or when the army was in bivouac, any time they could, they would hide some of them or they would give them things. But the moment the army found anyone, they would kill them. And many were killed.

Very soon the people realized that they couldn't stay because the army knew they were protecting the others. So when they heard that the army was coming, they ran into the mountains to hide. But some of the women had very small children and they couldn't hide very well. So the army found them, and over there where they found them, they killed them. The army went back and said that they caught such a number of *compañeros* of the guerrillas. But they were not guerrillas. They were women and children. And they were being killed. And many of the others, they just kept returning, and fighting and fighting.

Very soon the army came with tanks and they were bombing. We couldn't live in our houses anymore. And so the women came back to the houses, and the men didn't dare to come back. So the women were in the houses and they were working trying to get some food to feed the children as much as they could, but in most cases there was very little. Some of the men from time to time came down from the mountains to find out if there was anything for them to take. But they couldn't stay.

During this time the army came back every eight days, every fifteen days. Then the soldiers kept coming and saw the women without the men. "Where are your men?" they asked. We would tell them, "They are working the fields up in the mountains" or "They are working." Some of the women said, "We don't have husbands. We are alone." And the soldiers looked at the women, and said, "You are pregnant. Where are the men?" "They are not here." "We are going to kill you because you are lying," the soldiers said.

The soldiers realized that the women had brothers and husbands because they found clothing. So the women tried

> to hide everything, but the soldiers realized that they were scared and that they were lying. The soldiers told them that if they kept lying they were going to be killed and when the husbands and children would come back, they would find just the corpses. They told the women to tell the men that they were soldiers in ARENA, and they were in that area.

Torriera was getting upset with what she was hearing. "I think for her this is extremely painful," she said. "I don't think we have the right to hear her. She is really suffering, remembering all of that."

Carlota continued.

> They were already concentrated up in the mountains and the army found them and attacked the families with bullets and grenades. Many were killed. It was a miracle that the others escaped just by running away in between the bullets and grenades.
>
> On that day she lost six children. And she was running. In the next ten days she was able to come back to the houses with three of the children. Her daughter's children had run in different directions, and they remained in the mountains for ten days without food and hardly any water.

— 5 —

Next, Carlota's daughter Deema took up the narrative. She spoke of herself, as "her daughter." She was crying as she spoke.

> Her daughter worked with young children, and two of her brothers helped her move further away from the area. One of the leaders of the young men told her that she couldn't remain with so many young children because everybody would be in danger. They told her to get the children and live next to the road, so that after she would be able to return.

She was able to go to a man's house with the children. And the mother was able to reach that house and took the rest of her children, plus the oldest child of her daughter's. She remained in that house with the aunt with her child and baby. And the baby became very sick. The baby had measles. She was in the house and the baby died, and the father never saw the baby.

The mother had to leave this area because the soldiers were looking for her. So she went to a refugee camp with all the children. The daughter remained because someone had to stay with the father and the others. The daughter stayed there for over two months. And when the soldiers came, she realized that she had to leave also. After she left, the soldiers came and killed everyone in that house. Then they didn't know where to go. They went from place to place without having anything to eat. Until they heard about this community, and they came over here and they asked for help and to live in one of these houses, and that is how they came here.

When they came to this community, they started to feel much better because over here they found people who were trying to help them. In the beginning they were working with the men, organizing and everything and with other people also who were helping very, very much, and they started to make them feel much better. Now they have several places where they can work at different things, and the husbands and men in the community can work in construction. They have the capability that they could do work in construction. They have a building for carpentry, and a bakery, and many other areas they also can work in.

"I find it cruel," Torriera said. "We are causing these women pain when telling their stories. I think we should ask them if they want to continue talking."

"It is therapeutic for these people to tell their stories," the anthropologist said. Her small boy, bored with all the talking, fidgeted in his chair.

"Is your husband with you?" someone asked Carlota.

"My husband was for six years with the guerrillas."

"He was in charge of services," Blanchard interrupted. "In fact, he was with the commissariat. He worked for six years with the commissariat. Then he got arthritis, and he had to leave the guerrilla army and he came here with us."

"This is an interesting case, if you want to see an organized family in a community," Blanchard said. "That's Carlota, the mother, and these are her two daughters. Juana is the president of the seamstress cooperative. Her husband is the president of the *directiva* of this community. Her sister is the treasurer of the seamstress cooperative, and her husband is the accountant and storekeeper of the construction workers' cooperative. Her husband is from the same place, but they really got together here. One of Carlota's sons is in the carpentry cooperative and is the chief painter and is the secretary of the carpenters' cooperative, and the other brother is the treasurer of the construction workers' cooperative and the mechanic. Her cousin is the treasurer of all the social-pastoral projects. Her father is the president of the credit union. Everything that we buy for the cooperative we are putting in his name."

"This is an example of an interconnected family. Everybody is involved in some aspect of the organization. And that goes for her husband. Her daughter has now been incorporated into the carpentry shop, and her husband's brothers are either in the carpentry or in the scholarship program. I mean, you start going like this through the networks, and they go all over the place. Carlota was the Harriet Tubman. She and her mother made repeated journeys back into the mountains to rescue people. She has photographs of the different disguises. She has millions of stories about how they smuggled stuff in and out."

Blanchard stopped momentarily and looked at Torriera. "She does a great job," he said, praising her translating ability. "Even with some of the expressions that she could not know. Sometimes I have to work backwards when I'm translating."

"They are a family of twelve in this house," Ventura announced, "and their expenses are about one thousand colones a month. And it is very tight. They just about make enough money. They would like to go back to their original county where the land is better. But they cannot move because they cannot eat. They live day to day. But there is a desire to return to Chapeltique. They have some land there. They own a half acre."

"We went back a month ago, but it was bittersweet," Blanchard said. "It was a picnic, but it was going back to where the family had been killed. When we got there, the men could still climb the trees, but the children could not do it. They have lost some of their talents. They had become semi-rural. A generational shift has occurred. Carlota's sons will never go back, except maybe in old age to return to the farm."

I wondered about the people longing to return to their ancestral homes. Wouldn't that bother Blanchard after working tirelessly to build this community for them in Dolores Medina? Apparently, it didn't.

"Nema was one of the bravest young women in the community," he said, referring Carlota's other daughter. "Calle Real is in between Guazapa and San Salvador. If you want to use Biblical imagery. It's the distance between Syria and Egypt."

The Guazapa Blanchard referred to is a 4,620 foot jagged volcano, and during the war was a heavily bombed rebel stronghold in central El Salvador. The mountain's highest point was maintained by the army manning a radio station, while the lower ground was guerrilla territory.

"All of the armed forces were concentrated after 1984 when the FMLN continued to overrun their positions in the countryside," Blanchard said. "Nema went to a refugee camp, and she left immediately to enter into the war. She was recruited at the age of fifteen for what they call 'special operations,' which was going into places with dynamite, and stuff like that. She didn't like that, and she became a medi-corps personnel. And when they invaded Chalatenango, Nema led thirty young women across the mountain of San Salvador all the way to Chalatenango, all the way through those hills. Nema has absolutely no self-confidence. Nema thinks of herself as ugly, because she is brown-skinned. She thinks of herself as stupid because she is not educated."

"I don't know why you are telling us that," said Torriera.

"Because this is the double, triple poverty of the Salvadoran women. They are victims of poverty. And they are victims of their own self debasement."

I was shocked. Nema looked like a modern-day Madonna.

Chapter Twelve

Dolores Medina and the Cross

"You are very welcome in our community and in our parish for giving us the opportunity to let the rest of the world know about our history, about our situation, and about our dreams for the future. Because of our life situation here, we do not have many opportunities to let people know about our work."

We walked along a path toward the *carpintería* with a ravine below and a heavily farmed hill opposite. And rising in the distance, Guazapa volcano. The woodworking shop turned out to be a large, one-room building with a concrete floor and cinderblock walls.

"The people here are independent," said Blanchard as we stood outside. "They buy their houses, and this is the difference between an organized community and a disorganized community."

Inside the smell of cut wood filled the air. Several workers, young men and women, had assembled to meet with us, and scraps of lumber lay scattered everywhere, along with pieces of furniture in varying degrees of completion. Work benches held table saws, lathes, planes, vices, hand saws, drills, and hammers.

"The shop produces wooden craft items, furniture, and construction pieces, and sells them through a regional marketing cooperative," Blanchard explained. "Profits from the shop are reinvested in purchasing machines and equipment, and the remainder of the monies is used to help support the other services of the community, including a daycare center." The workers, he added, took full responsibility for all decisions of planning, production, and wages.

In one corner of the building was the paint shop, the area where "Gazoo" had worked, where designs were hand-painted on the crosses and boxes, readying them for market. In another section, cupboards and bureaus lay stacked on one another, along with a wooden bench with arm rests and a storage compartment under the seat.

"You could put a body in there," someone said.

A worker demonstrated how the bench opened into a bed.

"Members of the *carpintería* designed and built the piece of furniture by themselves," Blanchard said.

After touring the building, we sat on stools and chairs, and Blanchard asked the workers to talk about their jobs.

Rick Jones, who accompanied us from Carlota's house, translated.

"My name is Javier," said a young man in dungarees and a white, long-sleeved shirt. "I am the coordinator of the project here. We have three areas in which we work. The first one is furniture, and you can see a couple of pieces here in the shop. The second area that we have is carpentry. And the other is construction work that we do. We build windows and doors in buildings and homes whenever it is needed."

Another young man stepped forward. "I am responsible for the wood shop," he said. "We make crosses, wooden boxes for tourists, and furniture. Forty percent of our profit goes to the health clinic and to the daycare center. We know that someday we will have children, or that we will get sick, so we must support both of these programs. There are seventeen students working in the woodshop. The youngest is eight years old, and I am the oldest. I am twenty-one years old."

"My name is Oscar," said another. "I'm from LaPaz. I'm the secretary of the cooperative. This means that I'm in charge of the purchasing and I make sure of all the billing and receipts. We have three people who work mainly in building furniture. Most of the rest work in the woodworking and the artisanry or in the painting of it. And three people work doing construction. We are also part of a larger coordination of activities of other groups of carpentry shops and artisanries of various sorts that work in coordination with San Salvador, and we have two representatives who work with that coordination in terms of buying and selling to send stuff to the States. The coordination serves us so that we can have a market to sell what we produce here in the shop, whether it's furniture or artisanry. Through the coordination we have been able to sell our products to churches and to foreign markets, as well as to the delegations that come. You'll see there's going to be representatives from the various areas up in the *Ranchon* by the church later this morning."

"Where did you get the equipment?"

"Some of the things were purchased through grants from the refugee services."

"This is a planer," said Jones, pointing to one of the machines. "We were able to purchase that ourselves. We are still paying it off right now. Several of the other machines, the radial arm saw and the jig saws, were donated through a sister parish."

The workers wanted us to know about the amount of time they spent on the job, and explained it was not easy to become a member of the shop. A person had to apply for a position, and all the members of the *carpintería* voted on the applicant.

Also, to protect the shop from thieves they took turns sleeping on the premises at night. The community of Dolores Medina, they said, was not immune from crime because of the many ex-army people and death squad members living in the larger settlement of Calle Real.

— 2 —

Leaving the *carpintería* we walked back along the side of the main road, then turned up a dirt road that angled uphill to the right and was marked by ruts and small ravines. A large white building with two towers capped by large crosses sat on top of the hill. Half a dozen young girls clambered up and down ladders on an outside wall, painting a huge mural of white, black, and green two-foot tall houses with red roofs; trees with dark brown trunks and bulbous green canopies; huge tropical plants with multi-colored leaves; a rabbit with a white head, large green ears, a red torso; a man and a woman holding hands; and – arms outstretched over the scene – a twenty foot high Christ figure.

Blanchard was talking about finding places to sell items from the carpentry shop. "All we need is an outlet."

"We could sell them from the glass cases across from the language offices," Torriera offered. "I'm sure it is something that *La Hispanidad* would be interested in doing."

"When we get up here and you see the craft items," Blanchard said, approaching a building with an attached outdoor pavilion, "please don't think you are obligated to buy anything. These crafts are all made by the people in the community, and they are for sale, but they know you are not under any obligation to purchase anything."

The *Ranchon de Epifanía* was painted white, and the pavilion with its tiled roof supported by lengths of tree trunks housed several long picnic tables. A plant bed with red and yellow flowers ran its length, and to the left in the kitchen area a woman baked tortillas on an iron grill.

The tables overflowed with stuffed animals, hand-painted boxes, crosses, stacks of cards, handbags, tote bags, and men's and women's apparel.

"Would you believe this?" Bertsch asked. "The prices on these things?" She was holding a bunch of colorfully painted crosses and was so excited the crosses kept slipping out of her hands. "These will make wonderful presents."

McAllister picked out a blue short-sleeved shirt with "Oscar Rudolpho Romero" stitched over the pocket, and Kempton was busy stuffing a bag full of items.

While sitting on a ledge at the rear of the pavilion, I noticed a tall, thin man holding several letter size envelopes. We started talking and he said he was a Franciscan working for the summer in El Salvador.

"I taught at a Franciscan college back in the states," I said.

"Which one?"

"Siena. I taught there for five years."

"That's a different Franciscan province. How long will you be here in El Salvador?"

"Ten days."

"Could I ask a big favor of you? These letters. I wonder if you could mail them for me. The mails here are notoriously slow and inefficient. But if you could take them with you, and mail them when you get back to the U.S., that would be a big help."

He handed me the letters, and I placed them in my camera bag for safe keeping.

Members of our group, excited by the bargains, were purchasing armfuls of gifts when Blanchard interrupted, saying it was time to visit the health clinic.

"While we're inside, the women will prepare lunch for you. It's a surprise!"

— 3 —

In the health clinic we sat on benches in a small room, listening to three women health providers. Torriera interpreted.

"I am fifteen years old," said Marta, the youngest of the three, with long dark hair, dressed in jeans and a white T-shirt. "My job here at the clinic is to go to people's houses when they get sick. I am part of the diagnostic team. When people get sick I go to their home and take a sample of their feces. I look at the feces under a microscope and determine what is wrong with them, what type of bacteria they have. This way we will know if they need herbs, antibiotics, or something else. I learned this when I was in a refugee camp in Honduras."

Barker took notice of what Marta was saying, impressed especially with the door-to-door testing, and that she returned to treat patients until the parasites were eliminated. "There is much to learn and emulate from this simple, yet effective model of community healthcare," she said.

After the three women explained their roles, Blanchard turned to others in the hallway. Each said her name and briefly mentioned her responsibilities. As they gave their presentations, they reminded me of students talking in front of a class, wishing for all the world they were elsewhere. He had set them up, telling them we were university professors, and what they had to say was important for us to hear.

When the three women finished, Blanchard announced that the tables outside had been cleared for lunch.

"You won't believe what the women have prepared for you," he said. Now he was laughing. "They wanted to make something special for you, so they asked me what *Nortemericanos* like, and I said cook them whatever you want. Then they said, 'Do *Norteamericanos* eat pizza?' I said, 'They'll love it.' And you haven't tasted pizza till you've tried what these Salvadoran women cook up!"

Outside in the pavilion the women carried out large rectangular cooking tins filled with newly baked pizzas. Two of the women, dressed in aprons and white chefs hats, stood nearby, watching the proceedings, beaming. The trays were placed on the table, and we cut into the pizzas, thinking we'll have to make a fuss over this because these women tried so hard to serve us something that would remind us of home. Some of us were saying to ourselves, Salvadoran pizza couldn't possibly compare with Pepe's pizza in New Haven. Then we started eating. We were dumbfounded. The pizzas were delicious.

Blanchard got up. "Let me introduce the most extraordinary mother-daughter team in the world," he announced.

Torriera translated.

"Once again I want to give you greetings from the heart," Virginia, the mother, said. "You are very welcome in our community and in our parish for giving us the opportunity to let the rest of the world know about our history, about our situation, and about our dreams for the future. Because of our life situation here, we do not have many opportunities to let people know about our work. I speak basically from the point of view of the parish, but the dreams of the parish are also the dreams of the whole country. They are national dreams. In our parish, we have our projects that have been organized to work in the promotion of the community.

We were following the road, and we finally decided that the solution for us was not only to be found in the Bible, but also we had to find solutions to feed ourselves, from the point of view of the parish."

"From the parish," Torriera explained, "means everything is in the parish. OK? Whenever she talks, she is not talking about herself, but about the parish."

"In the parish they began to dream about different projects that would help make solutions for the life of the whole community," Virginia added, mentioning the carpentry shop as an example. She also talked about a sewing project making dresses for women.

"What we want," she said, "is to form a cooperative that will involve the idea of *mystica,* the dreams and spirituality of the whole community. We have other projects. The healthcare clinic, the daycare. But these projects don't bring in income. All the projects help the people to learn about a way of life that is good for the community. We hope that one day the people will be able to realize all their hopes and dreams, so their future will be secure. The people know that that is a difficult task, but we believe we will be successful. I'm part of the directive of one of the communities in the parish. A very important job of mine is to promote work inside the communities. I work with the other parishes of the archdiocese for CARITAS."

"People are helped to develop themselves in any way they want to develop," said Blanchard. "But the hope is to teach the person that their education is of great value to the whole community. Even as early as the Daycare Center, they try to include this idea because they realize that in their own lives this was not the case. So children are taught that it is much better to live as part of a community than it is to live alone."

—— 4 ——

Then Blanchard surprised us.

"The workers in the carpentry shop have a special gift for Sacred Heart University," he announced, "and they would like to present it to the group at this time."

Javiar, the *carpintería* coordinator, surrounded by several fellow workers, held a large, multi-colored wooden cross in his hands and presented it to Reid. Caught by surprise, Reid looked down at the cross, holding it waist-high with his left hand. The gift was totally unexpected. The rest of us, speechless, pulled out our cameras to record the moment.

"The workers hope that in the future," Javiar said, with Blanchard translating, "when the cross hangs back at the university, it will remind the Sacred Heart community of their connection with Dolores Medina."

Roughly three feet tall, the cross was covered with brightly painted symbols that, according to Blanchard, presented an overview of El Salvador's past, present, and hopes for the future. Javier pointed to two figures at the top, one dark-skinned, the other Caucasian, and explained, again with Blanchard translating, that the figures represented the sense of community that the people of Dolores Medina felt with the larger community of El Salvador and the world. At its base, stalks of maise, the life-giving plant of the Salvadoran people, grew out of four seeds symbolizing community, solidarity, peace, and justice.

Writing later in the *Sacred Heart University Review* about the symbols on the cross, Reid explained:

> At the intersection of the stem and arms of the crucifix is their rendering of the Sacred Heart. The left arm of the crucifix depicts their experience in the recently ended civil war: planes fly overhead, shooting, bombing, and destroying the people and the land below. The right arm contrasts the grim past with the people today – they are smiling, happy, and alive.[9]

Bertsch said it best. "They shared their bread and their lives with us, and they gave us the gift of love in the form of a cross."

Chapter Thirteen

The Army's Chief of Staff

"To be a citizen of a First World power has its costs, my friends. If you do not want to pay the costs, then leave."

After we left Blanchard and the people of Dolores Medina, we headed back to the city, hoping to catch part of the ceremonies honoring the war-wounded flown in from medical and rehabilitation centers in Cuba. People and cars packed the avenues around San Salvador's central plaza, and at first it didn't look like we'd be able to drive anywhere near the festivities, but Romeo smiled, as if to say *"no problema,"* and pulled out a large card that read "CNN Press," propped it on the front windshield of the van, and whisked us through several army checkpoints straight to the center of the activities.

By the time we arrived around 1:45 P.M., the celebration was in full swing. Music and speeches blared from loudspeakers. Red and white banners were draped over the lower face of the cathedral, and a platform with an awning, erected on the front steps, held the dignitaries. In the center of the plaza, the war-wounded sat in rows of seats facing the cathedral surrounded by throngs of well-wishers.

The war was over. The peace accords were taking hold. And in the Central Plaza, where years before people protesting the war had been shot and killed by the military snipers, a carnival-like atmosphere held sway, with the guerrilla war-wounded treated with all the pomp and ceremony of returning heroes. Vendors hawked hot dogs, sodas, FMLN T-shirts, banners and headbands, and long white banners were draped from light poles. In the crowds, people held aloft large red FMLN flags.

The atmosphere was infectious. I bought a red headband with "FMLN" painted in white lettering, and hesitated about wearing it, thinking it might be offensive to some FMLN sympathizers seeing it on a *gringo,* then decided it would be a sign of solidarity, and tied it around my head.

"I'm on the lookout for an FMLN cap," said Sacco. "For my son's collection. A cap from El Salvador would be a special trophy."

With speeches blaring over the loudspeakers, Ventura pushed through the crowds to the war-wounded where he managed to interview a veteran on his cam-recorder.

"This celebration will last well into the night," said Sacco.

— 2 —

The afternoon schedule called for a visit with the Salvadoran Army Chief of Staff at the military headquarters in San Salvador.

General Mauricio Vargas, a leading officer in the army, and the chief military negotiator in the peace talks, walked across the stage of the headquarter's auditorium and stood behind the podium, dressed in combat fatigues with his shirt sleeves rolled up. He stood looking at our delegation, his arms folded on his chest.

Ventura described the general as

> a man in his late forties (he asked for his reading glasses during his speech), in fatigues, polished boots, stocky, maybe 5 feet 6 inches, probably 180 pounds, a man who had certainly a high rank, though he did not wear any stars or medals, but who had an entourage of other people with stars and medals who looked up to him. They were always at his disposal, and would jump whenever he wanted something.[10]

"It is a pleasure and honor for us to receive you in the High Command," he said, speaking in Spanish, with Sinclair translating. "I am a general in the army, and I had the opportunity to work with the negotiations during the twenty-three months of working out the accords. First of all, we'd just like to hear your ideas on this report, or this conversation we are going to have. It's up to you, whatever you judge is most appropriate to discuss."

Trebon introduced himself, spoke about the purpose of our visit, and asked the first question.

> Q) What do you see are the positive things that have occurred, and what are serious things which must be done since the peace accords have been signed?
>
> A) First of all, I'd like to make a structure or a framework to talk about the peace accords. In El Salvador, there are two schools of political thinking. One school of thinking responds to the structural issues of the conflict which gave rise to the conflict. And the second school of political thinking is much more based on an interventionist ideology that the root causes of the conflict are owed either to the intervention of the United States, or Soviet Union and Marxist-Leninist ideology through the expansionism of Soviet Union, Cuba, and Nicaragua.
>
> We believe both schools of thought have validity. What we don't see as correct is that one school of thought is the dominant, isolating the other school of thought or legitimizing it. We believe that the two are interrelated, that there's an organic link between the two, and to the extent that they are addressed wholly makes for a better solution.
>
> If we were to analyze which of the two factors has the greatest influence or the greatest strength in causing the conflict, we would assess that it would have been the interventionist factor. And why are there two factors which gave rise to the conflict? First of all, this isn't theory, nor is it analysis. But it is objective reality which exists. It is based on practical life, and you can assess it from an historical perspective or from a practical perspective.
>
> In terms of history, we can look at two incidents in 1959 and 1979 which explain the typology of factors involved in the conflict. In 1959, Fidel Castro assumes

power in Cuba. And his thesis under which he took power was against dictatorship, against militarism, against colonialism, against underdevelopment. And thirty years later we have more dictatorship, more militarism, more colonialism because of the military bases inside Cuba. And we have equal or even worse levels of development.

And in the case Nicaragua in 1979, the fight against dictatorship, against militarism, against colonialism, and against underdevelopment, and for ten years they pushed Marxism anyway they could. They wear military uniforms and the military grows to a hundred and fifty thousand elements including popular militias. They have brigades of Soviet and Cuban military inside Nicaragua, and the level of development remains the same. These are the historic antecedents.

And in our country, the first offensive of the guerrillas to take power, takes place January 10th in 1981. During that uprising, there is evidence of submachine guns made by the Israelis, rockets from China. These arms were given by Cuba and Venezuela to the Sandinistas to overthrow Somoza.

El Salvador did not have military aid. El Salvador sustained itself against the revolution in 1981, 1982, and 1983 without military assistance. So this is the essence, the big sombrero under which everything else resides. The two types of factors: the structural factors gave rise to the conflict, as well as the interventionist factors. And I'm trying to explain why the interventionist factors predominate when explaining the nature of this conflict.

This explains why we see the interventionist factors as much more dynamic factors which led to the rapid changes that predominate over the structural explanations of the conflict, which granted were present but not in the same active form. These structural factors are utilized to engender political violence in the hopes of taking power.

And then we get to what is just a concrete fact, and that is the structural issues could have been changed. Let's go to a specific example. Changes in this country have been brought about by the peace agreements, and not brought about by the war. We have to be able to conceptualize the kind of country we want and to seek that country in the future, but we cannot accept the taking of power by way of arms.

And with that framework, now we can discuss more completely the peace agreements, which as of January 16, 1992 leave our country completely different, completely new. There are many Salvadorans who don't appreciate that we are living under a new stage of the republican life of this country. Why is that? I mentioned that there are structural problems. The peace agreements restructure the Armed Forces and put their mission in a new dimension. Public security is separated from the Armed Forces to a mission of more subsidiary action. The Armed Forces end up much smaller and very beholden to the civilian sovereignty of the country. The army's intervention in internal affairs is with only the exceptional. And only when the President determines it. That is to say, civil power determines the use of the Armed Forces.

Then we have the reforms in the judicial system. First of all, justice is no longer based on compliance with the law, but is now based on the philosophy of respect for human rights. And the composition of the Supreme Court of Justice will allow for the nomination of candidates that represent a pluralistic spectrum politically. That is named the National Council of Jurisprudence. They receive nominations for candidates and will make recommendations on those judgeships. Also there is a school of judicial training. This, in rough form, verifies what the judicial system involves.

We also have the electoral system. First of all, a Supreme Electoral Tribunal has been created, and within that are four different political lines or tendencies. There are those who believe in reforms to the electoral code and the revision of voter registration, and the whole political spectrum is represented. There is no other current faction that is not represented. Before the politics would go from the center to the right, but now it goes all the way to both ends of the spectrum.

Then we have the political participation of the FMLN, which enlarges the political spectrum of the country, and the cease-fire which is elemental to peace and the absence of all conflict. Also we have the process of verification by the United Nations, as well as a calendarization of execution. So the entire structure of the country has been changed, and all these structural changes are in the constitution and its amendments as of 1992. This includes all of the structural reforms contemplated within the parameters of the peace accords, as well as the creation of a human rights ombudsman.

So where has the progress or the advances been made through the peace agreement? We believe that compliance with the calendarization, which begins on January l6th and ends on the 31st of October, will be determined by the political will of those parties in agreement. The verification of the United Nations is very important, as well as the verification within El Salvador through the Committee on the Consolidation of Peace, known as COPAZ. Is that a response to your question?

"That's very helpful," said Trebon.

— 3 —

Next, this far-ranging Q and A session took place:

Q) As university professors we'd like to know your opinion on university education as part of the peace process.

A) First of all, one of the fundamental pillars that these changes really solidified comes through mentality and attitude, and every Salvadoran has to be changed. To change the mentality and attitudes of people, the basis of that is formation, education. One of the most important reforms has two different areas. One is structural, from the point of view of organic function, and the other would be a reform in the educational system.

We have, in terms of structure, the creation of a Military University. The second level is the center of studies for the Armed Forces in which all the studies of the military arts and sciences are discussed. The third level would be the Military Academy. And in this level there is a parallelism between military arts and sciences and academic military preparation.

We also have the basic training, or the center of training for our Armed Forces. Next we have training in small businesses and agriculture to help people participate in society. These changes should reach all twenty-one thousand kilometers and the five million people.

Why weren't structural changes important in El Salvador before? Because expansionism came to El Salvador first, so we had to ask the U.S. for assistance to fight against Communist arms. The U.S. responded very timidly in 1984. They began speaking with the FMLN in Washington because they did not think we would survive. I was in Congress and Senator Dodd said, "We'll help you, but I'll give you fifteen days before you fall." Now I'm a General and I will say to him, "What happened to those fifteen days?"

Q) Could the peace accords have happened eleven years ago, without all the fighting and bloodshed?

A) It is difficult to judge history. Especially when the facts have already been accumulated. It is not easy to do this kind of dynamic. But the polarization did not help or facilitate meeting the agreements.

Q) What happens to a people who have fought for a political mission half their lives? What sent new air into the discussions?

A) External factors played a major role. Who foresaw Dr. Gorbachev talking in the White House? It is not that the peace accords could not have happened, but the political polarization in our country did not allow for it. Yes, it could have been possible, but all the factors did not allow it to happen.

Man is a rational being. Facing limited resources with few means, people prioritize. The question of land is a very difficult problem. But it has to be answered in a rational fashion. Man has compensatory ways. We need to utilize the land better because there is not enough land for all the people. There is not enough for five million. But how do Saigon, Thailand, the Philippines, Hong Kong do it? We need to diversify, and we need to be very clear. We need training.

I don't want to say that we are not in a very difficult situation. But this is not immobilizing us. It must create a new solution. This isn't a simple problem. But I don't want to see the land as the problem of the country. It is an element of the historical dialectic.

In Guatemala it's the same problem, and El Salvador fits four times in Guatemala. Since the '60s, in Guatemala, Peru, the Dominican Republic, Panama, the revolution has been exported. But they have more land than they know what do to with. Maybe the U.S. will give us a piece of their land, and we'll annex it.

Q) Could you talk about plans to demobilize the military?

A) First, the reduction of forces is 50.2 percent of the total number of elements since the 31st of December, 1991. We are speaking of an average of thirty thousand men being demobilized – including security forces. What I can guarantee is that a new generation will come to write this history. No one in our generation can do this. Others, crazier than us, will change the history. But we will do it either because of necessity or because of conviction.

In November of this year, we will vote for a new Congress. Let me give a reflection, a very personal one. The U.S. is not present in Central America, Asia, or anywhere else for philanthropic reasons. They are there because it is in their interests. What happens? Its citizens must change their attitudes. They should understand what their president is doing. To be a citizen of a First World power has its costs, my friends. If you do not want to pay the costs, then leave. If you do not want to pay for who you are, then that is an error. This is your moment. The Cold War is over. This is your opportunity. You have the world in your hands. If it is too heavy, then drop it. Let it go.

Everyone must locate in the most objective terms the position of your country and the will of its citizens. I want to reiterate this. You are outside your country because your interests are there. In Panama you are there because of the canal, and not because of little black people and bananas. You are there because of natural oil reserves, and because of copper and silver.

In the present time, these relations will have to change. They are already changing with the Free Trade agreements with Mexico and Canada and Central America. The relations are changing and are interdependent. If El Salvador was helped it was because another Castro would have been here, and that would have impacted U.S. policy.

You are facing war. If you don't address it here, then you'll face it there. If you help here, it is not because you want to help a developing country, but because it will help you up there. Why is there so much crime up there? Because of the instability down here. That's my vision. We need each other with clear rules of the game, and with interests that are totally different. But together we can bring about a better world.

Q) Can you give us a breakdown in the formation of the National Civil Police?

A) The problems are of a difficult nature. First, there are problems which are not the responsibility of the government. Why are there these delays? We undertook a bilateral position. COPAZ is in a process of negotiations which are multi-lateral. In order to begin, you need a direction for the Police Academy.

Where does it start? COPAZ was delayed thirty-five days in the calendarization. The director was named thirty-five days late because COPAZ was late. Eight agencies in COPAZ must come up with the answers.

Secondly, there are problems with international assistance. For the peace process, the council was based in New York. The problem is eight hundred million dollars. Only sixty-three million has come four months after. And the calendar is half over.

The third problem is that the donors set up detailed conditions without knowing the realities of El Salvador. They say, "We'll bring a million hamburgers and French fries for the hunger of the *campesinos.*" But they want rice and beans. But the conditions say you must buy hamburgers and fries. And they must be bought out of the country. But how much does a Salvadoran meal cost versus a gringo meal? Also, bureaucracy holds things up because they feel the conditions are not being met. Right now a mixed group, including the FMLN, is in the U.S. talking about the problems.

Lastly, we have to recognize that we don't have complete trust. It is a process of ice which begins to melt. But sometimes it is our fears that don't allow us to move forward so fast. Last Friday, after speaking for thirty days with the leaders of the FMLN, we went over the problems of the delays. There are no more delays. We've solved those problems. But we've been saying all these bad things in the newspapers, and now we find they are not so bad.

Q) Will these problems still exist after the recalendarization?

A) People who don't read history are condemned to repeat it. We looked at the assistance in Panama and Nicaragua. They were promised large amounts of aid, but once their problems were over then forget about the aid. When someone goes drinking at night and wakes up the next morning he says, "I'll never go drinking again." And then when he's sober, he goes for the drink.

The international political community looks for problems elsewhere, and we have had that problem. For example in Panama, and then recently Chamorro was talking with Bush about moving ahead in Nicaragua. These are the reasons we are working on a continual basis. You are citizens privileged in the world. You can prolong or end these problems. And so what we are trying to do this afternoon is to discuss what is happening here and about the influence your country has on our country.

For example, how many of you were told that you were crazy to come here? But now you see that things are not that crazy. You can describe what the real problems are that face this country. And that is precisely what we did this afternoon. That you have a vision about our country. That the military are not savages, or a race of people from the Stone Age. They paint us as violators of human rights. But we want you to see the reality. Not what you read in the papers that have their own political agendas.

Perhaps when we get our military university, your professors could come here to teach. We thank you for your time. We are privileged to meet with someone of your stature. I have much respect for your government and your people. You should feel proud of what your country has done for our country. Time will tell. And this truth will be concretized in the development of our society.

As we trailed out of the auditorium, a couple of members of our group agreed that the general was "following the party line," while one other, reacting viscerally, called him "a stuffed shirt."

Had Vargas chosen his words carefully? No doubt. His job was to put a positive spin on the current situation for international visitors. But, at the same time, he did not hesitate to level charges at the self-serving policies of the U.S. Government, or hesitate to express his annoyance with what he called the misrepresentation of the Salvadoran military in the international press, or hesitate to register his chagrin with the perceived lack of the American electorate's resolve to help mend El Salvador's broken national reality.

He also agreed on the basics: the war had divided Salvadorans, and atrocities committed by both sides had caused deep-seated hatreds. But, he noted, there was hope for the future. Recent meetings when the two sides managed to talk were beginning to resolve some of the major obstacles to peace, so progress, slow in coming, was being made.

— 4 —

On July 13, less than a month after we returned home, the *New York Times* ran the following editorial:

El Salvador's Moment of Truth

> El Salvador has enjoyed a merciful but nervous peace since January, following a 12-year civil war that claimed more than 60,000 lives. The fighting ended with an agreement by guerrillas to lay down their arms and by the Government to discharge war criminals from a brutal army.
>
> An important milestone is fast approaching. On Aug. 15, a special commission will present its evaluation of the officer corps to President Alfredo Cristiani for possible purging. This long-overdue weeding-out deserves the full support of the U.S. government.
>
> The three commissioners, all respected Salvadoran civilians, came to Washington last week to meet with

officials and members of Congress. But they found that the bureaucratic wheels have turned slowly.

The State Department insists that it intends to share what it knows about notorious massacres, the murder of priests and of Archbishop Romero, and also about crimes attributed to leftist rebels. A full response, drawing on files of other agencies, would honor the cause of justice, and strengthen civilian scrutiny of a rough Latin army whose officers have had extensive U.S. training.

Past experience is cautionary. In December 1983, George Bush, then Vice-President, flew to El Salvador with a list of military officers believed to be involved in death squad atrocities. None were punished or discharged; the worst offenders were transferred to posts abroad.

Far more sweeping changes are envisioned in United Nations peace accords, which call for reducing by half the size of the army and for creating a national police force with guerrilla recruits.

U.N. monitors fault leftist rebels for seizing new farms after the cease-fire, and for providing lists of only a portion of the weapons they are supposed to surrender. But despite noncompliance by both sides, the accords have silenced guns to universal relief.

Exhausted belligerents show no wish to renew a stalemated war. And a war-wasted economy is reviving, helped by a wise U.S. decision to delay deportation of illegal Salvadoran migrants, prime source of $800 million in annual remittances.

It will truly mark a new era in El Salvador if the commission identifies malefactors, and Mr. Cristiani removes them as officers. Fuller cooperation in Washington can hasten that salubrious day.

Because of our session with General Vargas, I drafted a letter to the *Times*, printed Aug 6, 1992, under the headline "U.S. Can't Abandon El Salvador Now":

To the Editor:

I agree with "El Salvador's Moment of Truth" (editorial July 13), that our State department must cooperate fully with the Salvadoran civilian commission's efforts to evaluate the army's officer corps. It is to be hoped that President Cristiani, acting on the commission's report, will demand the purging of war criminals from the military's ranks.

Gen. Mauricio Vargas, the Chief of Staff of the Salvadoran army, met with our university delegation in San Salvador on June 17 and at that time said, "The peace accords restrict the armed forces, giving them a new mission. We are much smaller, and answerable to civilian authority." After Aug. 15 the world will know if General Vargas means what he says.

In the meantime, atrocities and violations of human rights continue in El Salvador after the signing of the peace accords, and the country's judicial system is failing to mete out justice. Police officials and judges, confronted with allegations of criminal actions are looking the other way.

Since 1981 our Government has pumped more than $4.5 billion into El Salvador, with $1.2 billion in direct military aid. Just because the cold war had ended and the threat of Communism has all but disappeared, we can't suddenly wash our hands of El Salvador.

Fairfield, Conn., July 21, 1992

Chapter Fourteen

The Massacre at the UCA

"They broke down that door and they entered in and pulled out the Jesuits. They brought them all out here, except for Padre Joaquín, who was sick. They assassinated him inside. And after they had them here, they fired."

"The UCA is a beautiful suburban university high up the slopes of San Salvador volcano, an oasis of civilized, affluent culture," wrote McAllister.

It also is the site of one of the most horrific episodes of the country's civil war: the gunning down by the military of six Jesuit professors at the university – known internationally as scholars, intellectuals, and outspoken critics of the army – as well as the slaughter of a housekeeper and her daughter.

The day of our visit we saw casually dressed students in jeans and short-sleeved shirts strolling to and from classes on tree-lined walkways curving around the university's buildings and manicured lawns. Unlike the University of El Salvador, its sister institution, where students were actively recruited to engage in the hostilities, at the UCA many students, insulated by class status and residing in guarded enclaves of the city, were largely unaware that a civil war actually was taking place. "As if it happened in another country," was the way Fr. Dean Brackley put it.

A handsome, lanky forty-six-year-old Jesuit, with a neatly trimmed beard and glasses, Brackley spent time with us explaining the role of the university in El Salvador's ongoing struggles for peace and justice. Ordained in 1976 as a member of the New York Province, he obtained a doctorate in religious social ethics from the University of Chicago's Divinity School, taught at Fordham University, worked as a community organizer in the South Bronx, and when the call went out in 1989 to take up the causes of the slain Jesuits, he moved to El Salvador where he administered UCA's School of Religious Education and became known for his advocacy of "the church of the poor."

— 2 —

It was late afternoon by the time we walked into the Centro Monseñor Romero building and turned down a long, narrow, white hallway, the walls filled with posters and pictures of Archbishop Romero and the assassinated Jesuits. In one framed set of photographs, Ignacio Ellacuría, the university rector, was in the top center; to his left Joaquín López y López, founder of schools for the poor; to Ellacuría's right was Segundo Montes, the chair of the sociology department; directly beneath Montes was Ignacio Martin-Baró, head of the psychology department; to his left were theology professors Armando López and Juan Ramón Moreno.

Another poster of the six Jesuits included photos of Julia Elba Ramos, the cook for the seminarians and wife of a caretaker, and her 16- year-old daughter, Celine Maricet Ramos, both murdered in a nearby cottage to ensure there would be no witnesses.

"You see books with their pages drilled by M16 bullets, shattered, bindings exploded," McAllister wrote later, describing the display cases in a small room at the end of a hallway inside. "You see what could be the debris of any professor's desk or pockets, and you see little glass cups, like dishes in a laboratory, full of dried blood and grass from underneath the bodies of the martyred."

Outside, behind the building, we stood behind a chain rope that kept visitors from trampling over small circular plots with pink, yellow, and red rose bushes commemorating the fallen Jesuits. We listened as Sinclair explained that the back of the building, pockmarked and splayed with bullets the night of the slayings, had been refaced and painted white, and in a corner to the right under a tree we viewed the black marble plaque on a large boulder etched with the names of the Jesuits.

We were talking in subdued tones, when a young woman joined us. Sinclair introduced her as Lilia Suarez, a secretary with the University. "She will explain what happened," he said.

Testimony of Lilia Suarez

> Among those who were here during the search was an ex-UCA student who was part of the Atlacatl Battalion. On November 16, probably between one and one thirty in the morning, the physical entry was through this gate here at the end of the walkway. But they also jumped over the fences back there. They encircled the area, because according to their own testimony, they didn't want the armed insurgents to escape.
>
> They broke down that door and they entered in and pulled out the Jesuits. They brought them all out here, except for Padre Joaquín, who was sick. They assassinated him inside. And after they had them here, they fired. And then on the way out is when they discovered the two women. The order was "no witnesses," so they ordered the killing of the woman and her daughter.
>
> After killing the people, they went into the offices here and destroyed the computer, typewriters, books, everything they could find. Most of them departed through the front gate, and left a little pamphlet there saying that the FMLN had done their justice. The next morning, the husband of the woman came and found the bodies. Julio, is a gardener here. The woman was the caretaker and cook. And then the investigation began.

"After they finished the steps of the investigation," Ventura commented, "closed chapter."

"The case is closed," Sinclair agreed. "It's just a question of whether the Truth Commission wants to resurrect it again. According to criteria for cases by the Truth Commission, cases that have been judged and finalized judicially will not be brought up. There's a lot of argumentation that says they didn't get the intellectual authors of the crime. That is, the High Command."

"Were they in uniform?" asked Sacco.

"Yes, they were," said Sinclair. "Everything except their insignias."

"How many military were involved?"

"Between forty and fifty," said Lilia.

"The military intelligence post is only about a half a mile from here," added Sinclair. "We're actually very close. It's just around the corner, right over the next hill."

"What about the UCA student who took part in the massacre?"

"He actually was one of the students," said Lilia.

"Only two people were convicted," Sinclair added, referring to the military officers convicted on September 28, 1991. "Colonel Venemedes and Lieutenant Shushi. Shushi was the student. Seven other officers were acquitted at the same trial."

"When they came in here, they fired for forty-five minutes," said Sinclair. "There were flares, there were mortars, they fired thousands and thousands of rounds of ammunition. And there was a military guard post real close to here, and there was no call that there was fighting here. There was no other kind of intervention. Representative Moakley has said that within the military there must have been collaborating. But there's no single official or soldier who volunteered any information on this case. Moakley, a Democrat from Massachusetts, spearheaded an investigation of the murders, and believed General Emilio Ponce, El Salvador's Defense Minister, was present when the order was given to kill the Jesuits."

But in spite of the "no witnesses" directive, Sinclair said, there was one woman, Lucia Cerna, who was in the area during the massacre.

"She lived in the house there," he motioned, pointing to the rear at a house behind a wall. "She was the only witness. She surfaced a couple of days after the events and went to the U.S. under

FBI protection. It created a real scandal when the FBI, instead of turning her over to the Jesuits as they had promised, kept her in seclusion in Miami for three days, interrogated her themselves, and then brought up a Salvadoran military officer to interrogate her. They repeatedly gave her lie detector tests until her story was so confused that she said she didn't see anything. And when she said she didn't see anything, then the lie detector test was false. So it came out that she was lying, and that's when Christiani and the State Department came out on record and said that she had failed the lie detector test, after they had forced her into a false testimony. She is still in the U.S. under the custody of the Jesuits who were furious over the treatment of the woman."

"What was the sentencing of the Colonel and the Lieutenant?" asked Sacco.

"Thirty years for Venemedes. Which is the maximum sentence allowable by the law."

"Why did they go after the Jesuits?"

"According to what we have seen," said Lilia, "there was an order to kill Ellacuría. Some of the testimony of the soldiers was saying, 'There is an enemy. He is the enemy. We have an enemy very close to us, and he's there in UCA,' which was Ellacuría. And this was right during the middle of the offensive. 'It's either us or them, and we don't want to leave any witnesses.'"

"I think I'm going to know the answer, but could you ask her to talk a little bit about why they saw Ellacuría as the enemy?" asked Reid.

"Because they always see someone as the enemy when they are constantly denouncing injustice," said Lilia. "And they are scared of those people who with their reasoning tried to solve the problems. I think the real hate against Ellacuría came when he would say the war could end if there was a dialogue. They were really bothered by the international support Ellacuría was getting for the positions he was taking."

An advocate for negotiations, Ellacuría at the time was urging rebel commanders to listen more carefully to what President Alfredo Cristiani was saying about ending the war. And later

Eduardo Sancho, one of the five rebel commanders, agreed. "Ellacuría said that Cristiani could be the way to negotiations. We didn't believe him."

When Lilia finished, she walked us past the back of the dormitory and administration buildings to a small house where the mother and daughter, Julia Elba and Celine, had hid during the massacre, and where the soldiers discovered and killed them.

— 3 —

After visiting the site of the massacre we met Dean Brackley on his way to class who said he would join us in front of the chapel around six for dinner. "Today I've invited a guest speaker to my class to talk about the Holocaust," he said.

With time to explore, we decided to visit the university bookstore, following slate walkways between academic buildings and stone steps leading from one level of the campus to another.

In the bright, airy bookstore, among several publications on the civil war and the peace movement, two booklets caught my eye: *Ciudad "Segundo Montes"* and *Los Acuerdos de Paz* – the former because of our scheduled visit in two days to the Segundo Montes cooperative in the northeastern province of Morazán, the latter because it would help to spell out and clarify the peace process.

Next we stopped at an outdoor cafeteria, a pavilion-like structure, which at 5:30 in the afternoon was packed with students, and quietly sipped coffees and sodas in the shade of overhanging trees. All of us were numb from the exhibits in the first building, the testimonies of Lilia and Sinclair, and the tour of the massacre site.

"Somehow after years have passed," said Sinclair, "the deaths of the Jesuits become sanitized."

Not for us.

Minutes later we stood across the street from the Centro Monseñor Romero building by cars parked on the side of the road, waiting for Brackley's class to end. That was when Sinclair mentioned that if we wanted to we could view the photos of the slain Jesuits.

"You don't have to look at them if you don't want to," he said. "But the pictures don't lie. Any of you who want to view the albums could do so. They show the bodies of the Jesuits blown apart by bullets. They are very difficult to look at."

All of us hesitated, asking ourselves what could we possibly see that our imaginations already hadn't conjured up. Was it even necessary? Were we guilty of a morbid curiosity? Did we have a responsibility to view the albums? Did we need more proof of what had transpired at the UCA?

But we were there. We had the time. So we walked with heavy steps across the road and up the sidewalk past stairs then followed another walkway to a glass door on the ground floor, conscious that we were about to come face to face with the abyss. Inside, behind a chest-high desk, a man quietly handed over the large albums and I took one, placed it on a nearby desk, and slowly began turning the pages.

The photos were horrific.

"These people," I wrote in my journal, "were ripped apart by automatic rifle fire, mostly to the head. The heads are shot up and totally destroyed. It is gut-wrenching, grotesque."

Whole sections of heads were missing, handfuls of brains strewn about on the grass.

"Some say the soldiers deliberately removed the brains from the skulls and threw them on the ground to signal their contempt for these men as intellectuals and professors," McAllister wrote in the *Sacred Heart University Review*.[11]

In the same place Bertsch wrote,

> I now recognize that with our visit to the Jesuit-run University of Central America (UCA), a limit of personal endurance was reached. I continued to participate, but my body ached and my spirit flagged. . . . On that brilliant, sunny afternoon at UCA, I was not prepared for the colored photographs of the bruised and mutilated bodies of the eight victims of atrocity.[12]

Sinclair stood nearby and I asked him about the cook, Julia, and her daughter, Celine. Photographs showed them sprawled on the floor, the mother lying on top of her daughter, as if in the terror of the moment she had been trying to protect her from the soldiers. Her skirt was torn away.

"The daughter was beautiful," I said, recalling the photo in the poster that showed her looking directly into the camera, wearing earrings, her face framed by dark, wavy hair.

"According to what I've heard, the mother was shot by a soldier who placed his rifle up her vagina," Sinclair said.

Back outside the building, Brackley met us briefly after his class. "You should check out the murals of the Jesuits in the chapel," he suggested, excusing himself to freshen up for dinner.

Yet more *memento mori*?

Inside the chapel a simple dark wooden table altar stood on the floor of the sacristy, and behind the altar a large wooden cross was covered with painted images of Salvadoran people, maize, and houses. Two large paintings on wood also filled with Salvadoran iconography hung to the right and left of the cross. Then as we turned to leave we saw the life-size murals of the slain Jesuits on the rear wall of the chapel.

"On that brilliant, sunny afternoon at UCA," wrote Bertsch, "I was not prepared to defend all sensibility against the Michelangelo-like, life-size drawings of the dead on the walls of the college chapel. And I began to despair."[13]

— 4 —

It was close to 7 P.M. by the time we arrived with Brackley at an open-air restaurant in the city.

"There will be music," warned Sinclair, "but we're hoping it won't be too loud."

While we ate, Brackley, pressed for time, launched into a talk about UCA, the slain Jesuits, and the current political situation in El Salvador. But as if on cue just as he started speaking the band struck up, horns blaring. It was impossible to hear Brackley. Out of desperation, he got up from his seat, perched himself on a railing behind us, and started shouting over the music.

"UCA is involved with the liberation of the poor," he said. "The school pursues the truth while confronting the systematic lies perpetrated in the country."

Basically, he said, the three university programs – social projection, teaching, and research – all were dedicated to furthering the pursuit of truth. The social outreach program projected into the public forum, and included all areas that reflect the social consciousness of the university. "The social outreach program must guide the university's research and teaching," he said. "UCA would like to help shape the social consciousness of the people."

The program, Brackley said, required students to perform six hundred hours of social service before graduation. But the requirement, in some instances, fell short of its goal. "The concept looks good in the school catalog, but the actual program had some serious flaws." For one thing, he said, students put off performing social services until later in their academic careers, which meant undergraduates failing to reach junior or senior year never participated.

Even with its flaws, the program brought up an intriguing question. Could community service be required on our campus? An integral part of the university experience at Sacred Heart since its founding, service was required by the charters of all clubs and organizations, but was not part of an institutional-wide mandate. That meant the majority of our students missed out on the opportunity to serve the larger community. At the very least, making service, if not a graduation requirement, more accessible to our undergraduates, needed serious consideration.

"The UCA's principal subjects of study," Brackley said, "are the national reality and the social reality. At UCA we study the world. But the overriding question is, how are our studies going to serve the truth in this country? It is really challenging. We live within an intellectual climate of distortion. And our students come to us living in a world that is part true and part false. Our problem is to explode that eggshell. This is a country that runs on lies. Domestically we are involved in a struggle for the truth. For example, when I arrived in 1990, a survey was published in which the plurality of the people said that the FMLN was responsible for the majority of the atrocities. How could this happen?"

"Most of the people are functionally illiterate, and then there was a massive promulgation of lies by the government. Add to that the fact of state terror, and you begin to understand how such a poll could be published. Basically we have a war of the oligarchy against the poor. You figure basically everyone knows the truth. You visit Calle Real, and that is the cutting edge of the dialectic of history."

To help fulfill the pastoral mission of UCA, Brackley pointed out that each Jesuit worked in a poor parish in the countryside as part of the social projection orientation. "Where I work," he said, "the people are so afraid that they still refuse to speak. Twenty people died there during the civil war. If I am a *campesino*, state terror makes it impossible for me to talk about my life, my work, and my family history. The apparatus of state terror must be dismantled, and it will happen incrementally and dialectically. There is right now, before your eyes, a public dispute with ARENA. Christiani goofed up on the death squads and the army. The death squads must be stopped. One death makes it impossible for people outside the city to organize." But, he added, the climate was slowly changing. People were beginning to believe in the possibility of a new order in El Salvador.

"Many people would argue," Brackley said, alluding to the death of the Jesuits, "that the end of the war would not have occurred if the massacres had not happened. That event woke us from our bipartisan slumber and embarrassed Congress. It turned into an important element that brought the military to the point where the accords were made possible. And we kept that emphasis alive."

The answer, he concluded, was to be found in three words: "truth, justice, and reconciliation. Of course, we Jesuits can speak forever, so now I'll keep quiet. And of course," he smiled, "we don't live up to all this."

— 5 —

That night a few members of our group returned to the Central Plaza in the city to take part in the ongoing celebration for the war-wounded, a revelry that promised to last till dawn and beyond.

"Wounded guerrillas in combat fatigues and the people of San Salvador in FMLN red T-shirts, headbands, and hats, hugged one another and danced in the plaza," said Sacco.

That was where he met Deimas. "He had been shot in the leg, and after he was operated on and his leg stretched eight centimeters, he still limped."

"But not as much as before," Deimas told Sacco.

"I asked him where I could get a hat like his. He took off his hat, signed it, dated it, then handed it to me. I offered him money, my expensive Guayabera shirt, even my shoes, but he refused everything. Later I told him our delegation was visiting the Segundo Montes cooperative in Morazán on the weekend. Deimas said he too was going to Morazán, and he might see me there."

Chapter Fifteen

Women's Rights and UES Dialogues

"Crimes like rape and incest, especially in the countryside, are rampant. But the biggest issue facing women is their lack of self-esteem, compounded by the fact of the ever-present machismo among men. And the fact that most women are illiterate."

At 6:45 Thursday morning, Sinclair convened a "power breakfast" to go over the two scheduled sessions for the day. The first, a meeting with Maria Esther Chamorro, a women's rights activist, would serve as an introduction to issues surrounding the role and status of women in El Salvador. Primarily, this would be an interview session. The second meeting, scheduled for the afternoon at the UES, was more complicated.

"The university people are looking for experimental dialogues," he said, "and are hoping for more significant academic exchanges at a later date."

The proposed meetings, set up in three sessions, would investigate four broad areas: anthropology and history, marketing for agricultural cooperatives, alternative media and communication channels, and issues affecting women in education. Members of our group could decide which of the four areas they felt most qualified to discuss. The first session would entail a sharing of concerns; the second session would arise out of the first session; then a third part would be set aside for participants who wanted to draft proposals for a follow-up.

"I tried to define agendas," Sinclair said, "but I'm not sure what is going to happen. So there's no pressure to participate in these meetings. I wouldn't want you to feel that way. Any of the meetings could be cancelled. So this is not something you have to prepare for. If the meetings don't pan out, there would be no hard feelings."

Stomach cramps hit with a vengeance soon after breakfast, the result of something I had eaten or drank the night before, so when the group left to meet with Chamorro I stayed behind, hoping to pull myself together for the university sessions in the afternoon.

"No matter how thirsty I am," Torriera said, "I always put the iodine pills in first, and wait ten minutes, and then take a drink. And so I am not sick."

Willison, Spence, and myself were supposed to get together with journalism faculty, and before the group left for the morning session, Willison said if I wasn't feeling better, he could pinch hit for me that afternoon. "I was a journalism major," he said, "and served as advisor to a high-school newspaper."

Back upstairs I tried brainstorming ideas to hand over to Willison, but faced questions with no answers. What was the role of the student press in a atmosphere of fear and repression? What about UES students and faculty being jailed? And death squads roaming the streets? Was freedom of the press even on the table?

— 2 —

The morning session took place at 11 A.M., and covered a far-ranging set of issues facing women in El Salvador, including problems with self-esteem, illiteracy, rape, harassment, children born out of wedlock, and overcoming resistance to change. The session was taped, and later transcribed.

Maria Esther Chamorro Talk

I am very sad that my English is not so good, because I have not spoken very much for a long time. I visited the

United States when I was a little girl, from three to eight years old, in California. I learned the language when I was so little.

I studied in Connecticut, in 1960-1961. I went to Connecticut College for Women in New London, Connecticut, and I was in an exchange student program. Here I have been teaching in many schools. Secondary schools. And I also studied at the International University.

Right now I am involved in a women's project which is called "The Women's Citizens." This is a new project which works with women in the community and helps them defend their rights, and helps them participate in an affirmative way in the new democratic life of the country. It is not possible yet because we are in the planification stage, and a new person is going to come now to start to manage some of the problems.

I am very sad that my English is so bad. Now it is a little bit rusty because I haven't practiced very much. Sometimes when I practice a lot, it is too much like my own language Spanish, because I learned it when I was so little.

I was in the National University in the 1970s. There is a big difference in the National University from 1973 to 1975 and the way it is right now. They had a lot of military intervention, and fighting inside the university. It is very sad what happened.

And right now the new rector is Fabio Castillo. I think he's a good man who can bring back the university to what it was before, several years ago. He's a very strong man. He is really working. He's very strict. And I think that he can really bring back the university, and that is why it needs a lot of support. I want to give support to the university. And I am still thinking of taking part in it because they were my companions years ago, and they gave a lot of their support.

At this point, Torriera mentioned the donation she planned to make to the UES.

"In our department," she said, "we are getting a brand new language lab. But the one that we have now is Sony equipment in perfect condition. I asked about donating the lab to the University of El Salvador, and was told that that was a good idea. It would be best in that university."

"That is good," Chamorro said. "Yes, they must be very happy."

> You know the university had a very good program to qualify their teachers. My husband in 1971 went to England to work in a program of study by the National University. It was a family program, because we went with one child. Now they need a lot of support. That's why people from here have been connected with them. They have a group of people, national people that will help them. That is why I really want to continue our relations.
>
> The women's subject is a new subject. It is something that maybe has developed in the last three or four years. Maybe the last two years. Right now we have the commitment to help women in the communities. A lot of organizations come and they give their ideas.
>
> There is a lot of sifting and prioritizing that has to be done. For example, crimes like rape and incest, especially in the countryside, are rampant. But the biggest issue facing women is their lack of self-esteem, compounded by the fact of the ever-present *machismo* among men. And the fact that most women are illiterate.
>
> Another concern is the illegitimate birth rate, and the large percentage of births that take place in the home – either because of lack of money to pay for hospital care, or because of the distrust of hospitals. In general, there is resistance to change on the part of both men and women. But the women's movement is a popular movement, with strong participation in women's organizations throughout the country. They are preparing right now for the World Meeting of Latin American Women.

Among the issues Chamorro identified, the central concern, the lack of self-esteem, was the same issue Blanchard alluded to at Dolores Medina. That, plus *machismo* and an ingrained resistance to change, suggested that the struggle for women's rights demanded a nationwide cultural shift that would take years to develop.

— 3 —

A few days before we left for El Salvador, Reid had received the following letter from Sinclair outlining the proposed UES sessions:

> 1. *Methodology of Investigative Field Work in Anthropology and History.* They would like to dialogue both about the concepts (what is the notion of anthropology, is it a science, who are the objects of study and what problems that poses, problems of prejudices of the observer, what is the purpose of anthropology) as well as what are the steps in the investigative process. Their interests are much more specific on this session (they gave me a ten-page document!) and are really looking for assistance in designing and implementing a longer training course. They are looking for donations of bibliographic material as well as support for an investigation of repopulated communities. I will go over this more with this group upon your arrival.
>
> 2. *Issues of Marketing for Agricultural Cooperatives.* The UES does technical agricultural assistance (irrigation, ag inputs, etc.) for cooperatives but little in terms of theories of finance and marketing for cooperatives. Their interest would be both about domestic markets as well as international markets. Again, they ask for more of a methodology of investigation, the steps on how they should investigate and learn, rather than compress complex theories into a short session.

3. *Developing Alternative Media and Communication Channels.* I did not meet with anyone from this group, but I imagine their concerns are with teaching journalism, photography, and video in a university setting under grave limitations (lack of equipment, lack of freedom of press). Their interests would be not only technical but also theoretical: how to use the media to open political space, the tension between advocacy reporting and objectivity, what political pluralism means within media.

4. *Issues Affecting Women in Education.* Again, I did not meet with anyone from this group, but their concerns were relayed to me. Our counterpart will be MUES [Women from the University of El Salvador]. They are very interested in learning about the struggle in the U.S. to have "Women's Issues" become a curriculum of study in a university setting. They also are interested in developing a "University for Rural Women" to educate women on domestic production, nutrition, literacy, political organizing.

"Please," Sinclair insisted before the group left the hotel, "do not get anxious about this. These are not formal sessions. Rather they are an attempt to bring academics together from different backgrounds to share their mutual interests."

— 4 —

The reviews on the afternoon UES sessions were mixed. Two of the first round meetings proved fruitful, while the other two ran into difficulties. Locating people, finding places to meet, then responding to the specific needs of the faculty was a struggle.

Ventura's group asked for specific information about farming cooperatives. But since he was not an authority in that field, he said he could speak only in general terms. Willison was prepared to talk about journalism and Spence thought she would be discussing film theory and history. Instead the media profs talked about their lack of equipment and lack of editing experience, and wanted instruction on pulling together extensive collections of raw footage of the civil war. In an attempt to salvage the meeting, Spence agreed to ask Professor Rebecca Abbott, an experimental film-maker at SHU, if she would be willing to travel to El Salvador to help make sense of the wartime footage.

The "Women's Issues" meeting, attended by Kempton, Bertsch, and Sacco, met with better success. Their session held with medical and science personnel covered a broad range of topics, including enhancing the status of women and developing women's consciousness.

"You begin within yourself," said Bertsch on the latter topic, "developing a sense of your own inner worth and well-being."

As a result of this meeting, the UES women forwarded papers they had developed to the hotel for Kempton, Bertsch, and Sacco to review and comment on.

After dinner that night at the *Cafe de Don Pedro*, the restaurant we visited on our first night in San Salvador, the main topic was the next day's trip to Morazán and Segundo Montes City. For security purposes, we'd be traveling in two vans.

"It will be at least a four-hour trip if all goes well," Sinclair warned. "The bad news is the closer we get to our destination, the roads will be in poor shape because of past military clashes. The good news is we'll make pit stops along the way."

With several of us under the weather – Reid recovering from stomach cramps, I feeling so-so, Barker and Willison beginning to feel sick, and Bertsch's back acting up – driving to Morazán cooped up in vans for hours was not an appealing prospect. But no one wanted to stay behind.

"I wasn't able to visit Morazán before because of the fighting," Sinclair said. "We'll be based in the community, and you can expect other international visitors staying there. There will be no running water, and no electricity where we'll be staying, and we'll be housed in dorms. But the shower facilities are better," he said, grinning. "You'll have a bucket of water to throw on your heads."

Also, he mentioned that Chester Wickwire, the retired professor from Johns Hopkins we met earlier, might hitch a ride with us.

5

By 11 o'clock the next morning we piled our gear in the lobby, about as ready as we could be for the junket to Morazán. Joining us, his crutches leaning against the lobby desk, Chester Wickwire stood arms folded across his chest, an embroidered shoulder bag draped over his hip, a small black EMS container hanging from his neck, wearing a cap with the insignia "This Old House WGBH."

"I've led several groups down here over the years," he said, sitting on the lobby sofa. "The Faculty for Human Rights in El Salvador is a network of academics. From 1979 we brought lawyers, doctors, and professors, especially to El Salvador in the beginning of the war. I have been going to Guatemala, Nicaragua, and Hondurus. We tried to speak to people in business, the military, and economics."

"Sounds like what our group is trying to do."

"Yes. Very much. I come down here an average of three or four times a year. Basically we've tried to help political prisoners, the professors and teachers who have been thrown in jail. We were pretty effective in helping people. We worked with Congress, trying to get some changes in our government's stances on Central America. We've been pretty bad down here. I also worked in Nicaragua, taking Somoza and introducing him to Congress. And then we've done some TV shows back in the U.S."

"Maybe you could talk to us about what we should be doing when we return to the states," I said. "Part of the reason for our trip is for us to become more effective lobbyists supporting peace initiatives and human rights in El Salvador."

"I'll be happy to share ideas with you."

At that point Sinclair was explaining why we were traveling in two vans. "We're driving into the mountainous northeastern sector of the country. The two vans are for security reasons and comfort."

After the war, he said, even with the accords in place, the countryside was dangerous. Precautions had to be taken. The familiar mantra was, "Stick together, watch for anything suspicious, and don't draw attention to yourselves."

Meanwhile McAllister scanned the lead story in the San Salvador daily paper linking a Sandinista arsenal of munitions with the FMLN.

"It's not quite clear whether they discovered these arms here in El Salvador or in Nicaragua," he said. "The government forces discovered an underground cache of arms for roughly four hundred men in the house of FMLN leaders in Nicaragua."

Chapter Sixteen

The Road to Segundo Montes

On a flat area at the top of the hill, a large L-shaped open-air pavilion offered a commanding view of the surrounding countryside. Inside several men and women, some dressed in combat fatigues, sat at long picnic tables. It was a conference of rebel leaders.

The drive to the mountain village of Perquín in the northern sector of Morazán took us through the province of San Vincente and the northern part of Usulután.

Close to one o'clock, Sinclair called for a stop at a gas station overlooking the four-lane road divided by a median strip of grass. At the time, it felt like a handful of sand was grinding away at my stomach walls, so I elected to stay put in the van with Willison, Barker, and Sacco.

Across the road a convoy of six large, open-backed trucks packed with uniformed soldiers stacked together came to a halt and several jumped out to stretch their legs. Four car lengths behind was the required escort, a white United Nations van.

"It's the job of the U.N. peace-keeping forces to oversee the movement of any troops in the country," Sinclair explained.

Back on the road, we traveled another two hours, stopping for lunch at an open-air cafe under a stand of trees. Diners sat at tables under a tin roof, and inside was a large enclosed room, a kitchen area, and restrooms. Across the street an imposing walled-in compound topped by sentry boxes, was the base for the army's 3rd Battalion. Sentries in camouflage fatigues, sleeves rolled up to the biceps, carrying automatic rifles guarded the entrance.

"This should be quite a hot spot," Willison observed, checking out the cafe. "Look inside. There's a dance floor in there. This must be quite the place on a Friday night when the guys from the barracks get off duty."

Over drinks and spaghetti, conversation turned to a notorious incident from the war. Gradie was talking about Lieutenant Colonel Domingo Monterrosa, a legend among government forces, and the charismatic leader of the Atlacatl Battalion. Known for tearing babies from their mothers and hurling them into burning ovens, he was the commander responsible for the El Mozote massacre that began on December 11, 1981, when close to 700 people were slaughtered. At the time, government officials in the U.S. and El Salvador denied reports of the massacre, and reporters for the *New York Times* and the *Washington Post* were denounced by right-wing critics for what were construed as their biased accounts of the carnage.

But the reporters were vindicated when Rufino Arrayo, the sole surviving eyewitness who lost four children and her husband, recounted the story of the massacre. According to her account, after shooting and decapitating the men, the soldiers raped the young girls of the village, shot the mothers, then strangled and cut the throats of children who had taken sanctuary in the village church.

Later, it was said that the guerrillas exacted revenge for Monterrosa's atrocities when he climbed aboard a helicopter booby-trapped with a rebel bomb and the copter exploded in mid-air.

2

Closer to Morazán, at one point Sinclair told Romeo to pull over. We climbed out of the vans and stood by the side of the road, entranced by a vista of lush, green farmlands divided into plots and stretching off into the distance and up the side of a mountain. As far as the eye could see the land was under cultivation.

"This is good farmland, owned by wealthy families," mused Sinclair. "Most *campesinos* know nothing else but farming. And with not enough land for everyone, part of the economic future of the country rests in training people to work in light industry or other occupations."

But the maquiladoras, the huge factories where *campesinos* sought employment, were rife with poor working conditions, long hours, and low wages, he said. Stories abounded about the workers attempting to organize and about the abusive measures of wealthy owners hiring and firing at will.

After San Miguel, the last major city before entering the province of Morazán, we drove northeast following the Rio San Francisco past the town of San Carlos and finally stopped for gas at the town of San Francisco Gotera, the entrance to what during the war was known as "the red zone."

"This place was the last stronghold of the government army," Sinclair announced. "The population of this town swelled by some ten thousand people during the war because of the presence of the army and refugees. This is uncharted territory for me. On previous trips this area was too dangerous to travel to because of the ongoing conflict."

Reminded again to exercise caution for safety's sake, my imagination flipped into overdrive. Across the street from the gas station a group of men stood watching us milling around, and I imagined them getting angry at two vans of *Americanos*.

It was McAllister who later objected to characterizing any situation as threatening. "I was never, never, never made to feel uncomfortable as an American," he said in the drive from the airport back to the university.

Meanwhile, the other driver was pushing against the side of his van, rocking it back and forth.

"What's he doing?"

"Trying to get as much gas into the tank as possible."

— 3 —

A light afternoon rain fell as we drove north toward the Torola River past the village of Chilanga and up to Yoleciquin where the Rio San Francisco veered off to the left. Bertsch, writing later in the *Sacred Heart University Review*, captured the beauty of the landscape:

> I was awed by the presence and power of the hills and the mountains, the volcanoes and the rocks – the arena in which the people of El Salvador had fought, to which many were forced to flee and from which many "disappeared" – the mountains that so often were hidden by the clouds, enveloped in the early morning mist, or covered during intense tropical storms as if by a sheet of smoked glass. They were startling in their powerful and merciless beauty. [14]

Beyond the village of Delicias de Concepción, in a matter of minutes we came upon the Torola, a brown ribbon of water that edged the southern border of Honduras and the northern part of the province of San Miguel, then flowed east through the guerrilla-held mountains of central Morazán. During the war, anywhere north of the Torola the civilian population was believed by the army either to be active in the rebel ranks at least supportive of their cause.

We drove up to a lengthy dilapidated bridge spanning a gorge with the river far below. Considered a strategic link to the North, the bridge was blown up several times during the fighting and, in spite of the cease-fire in effect, rightist sympathizers recently planted a grenade, blasting out a mid-section to impede traffic and the flow of supplies to the rebel stronghold of Perquín. Logs were thrown over the damaged section so vehicles could attempt to pass, but the rain made the wood slippery and the churning wheels of vehicles left gaping holes.

Romeo stopped the van and got out to check the makeshift repairs. Deciding to give it a try, he got back in, shifted into first gear, and plowed forward, sending the van bouncing and lurching as the tires spun over loose planking and logs. Halfway across the right front wheel slipped through logs, dropped about a foot, and the van came to a sudden stop, leaving it tilted on an angle.

Inside we held our breaths while Romeo opened the driver's door, found some secure footing, and stepped out to survey the damage. Meanwhile a dozen children, excited by the spectacle, ran up to watch the unfolding drama. At that point, Sinclair and the folks on the passengers' side of our van managed to open the doors and pick their way to the solid planking of the bridge.

I slid back the door on my side, and looked down. Between the logs, wet and spun out of place, I could see the brown water of the river far below. The logs, up to a foot in diameter, had been placed side by side on top of 2 x 6 inch steel girders running a foot apart under the planking of the bridge.

I managed to wedge myself out the door, stepped carefully on the logs, slid the door shut, and made my way over to the front of the van. The front wheel on the passenger's side was wedged up to the axle between the steel girders about eight feet from where secure planking started again. After assessing the situation, we grabbed the front end, lifted the wheel free, pushed the vehicle back to the solid planking, then rearranged logs to cover the damaged spot. At that point Romeo climbed into the van, backed up, stepped on the gas, and tore across the repaired section with the logs clattering beneath the wheels and flying in all directions. With the van safely on a secure section of the bridge, we jumped back inside and sped across the rest of the way without incident.

— 4 —

We drove past a large government encampment in a field under trees, and into Segundo Montes City, a community under the protection of the FMLN named after Fr. Segundo Montes, one of the assassinated Jesuits who founded the Human Rights Institute at UCA [IDHUCA] and was noted for his work with Salvadoran refugees.

By now the afternoon rain had stopped and in a yard behind a row of shacks a gathering of about thirty people sat and stood in a large semi-circle watching a TV perched shoulder-high on a platform above the ground. Some people stood as far as twenty feet away, craning their necks to get a better view of the screen. I had no idea what the program was about, but they stood in the dusk watching and listening, captivated.

Past an open market, the vans climbed a dirt road up a hill winding through heavy vegetation and one-story concrete block buildings to a flat area at the top where a large L-shaped open-air pavilion offered a commanding view of the surrounding countryside. Inside several men and women, some dressed in combat fatigues, sat talking at long picnic tables. It was a conference of rebel leaders.

Sinclair went to find the welcoming committee, and we walked over to the edge of the parking area to a sharp drop-off. Far below dwellings lay scattered among the trees with several foundations under construction, and beyond the houses a rugged, hilly countryside gave way in the distance to mist-covered mountains.

Back at the pavilion we gathered around a table where a woman explained we had to officially sign in, drop off our gear at the dormitories, then return to the pavilion for supper.

Following instructions, we walked down the dirt road to a small white building where we signed the Segundo Montes guest book.

"There's a rule when travelling," Wickwire advised, spying bathrooms behind the building. "Never pass up a *baño*." With that, he picked his way around the side with his two canes.

Outside I heard shouting. Across the road two cinderblock shacks nested among the trees below, and a man was standing by the nearest shack, about twenty-five yards away, yelling and throwing stones at a skin and bones dog cowering in a small garden. A young boy, probably the man's son, stood nearby, watching, while a pig and half a dozen scrawny chickens rummaged in the dirt close to the shack. Soon a stone found its mark and the dog yelped and ran off, tail between its legs.

Sinclair had warned us about the treatment of dogs. How in poorer communities, rather than "man's best friend," they were viewed as pests competing for the little food available. Accustomed to dogs as pampered pets back home, it was difficult to watch

Salvadoran dogs, ribs visible under mangy hides, slinking around. We didn't see many, but those we did were not welcome.

— 5 —

Once plans for the evening and the next day were arranged, we drove back down the hill, climbed another plateau, and stopped in front of two one-story, dormitory-style, rectangular wooden buildings. Behind the buildings, the land remained flat for a couple of hundred feet, then dropped off to the valley. On the other side of the road on higher ground under trees was what looked like a small village of blue, red, and green painted shacks.

The women, Ventura, and Wickwire carried their bags into the dorm to the left, while the rest of us piled into the other one. Roughly thirty-five feet long and twenty feet wide with dirt floors, the buildings came with metal cots, folding chairs, a card table, and thin mattresses. After we decided who would sleep where, I set my pack under a cot by the door and walked outside and around back to check the showers Sinclair had mentioned earlier.

Three small open stalls with tin roofs attached to the back of the dorm had floors of flat circular stones and each stall held a fifty gallon drum filled with water. The idea was to strip, ladle water out of the drum, pour it over yourself, scrub yourself down, douse yourself again, then towel off. Beyond the showers, a path led to another building and I poked my head inside. The community *baño* was equipped with three primitive concrete toilets, plus an overpowering stench.

Retracing my steps, I met a young German couple in front of the dorm, tanned and athletic-looking in hiking boots, khaki shirts, and shorts. They spoke English and said they were touring the country "on vacation." I was dumbfounded. With its scars from the war and current unrest, El Salvador hardly seemed an optimum spot for a vacation.

That evening we drove back to the pavilion for supper, stood single-file in front of the counter to pick up our chicken, rice, beans, and drinks, then moved to the long picnic tables where members of the rebel army sat eating. Wickwire, not passing up the chance to learn the latest about the unfolding peace process, sat at the end of the table, talking to a bearded fellow dressed in army fatigues. I wished I knew what they were saying.

Talking to Wickwire later, I forgot his chat with the rebel, and instead asked him what he thought about the military's role in the UCA massacre.

"It doesn't make sense to me," I said. "I understand the part about how they hated the Jesuits, but why would they get involved in a massacre? I know they left leaflets trying to point the finger elsewhere, but they must have suspected that the operation could backfire and the truth would come out."

"I think the FMLN offensive had them in a panic," he said. "The people were saying they were 100,000 strong, at least with their sympathizers included."

After we finished supper, while a heavy early evening rain enclosed the pavilion in cascades of water, Sinclair filled us in on the program for the next day: a tour of ongoing projects at Segundo Montes, then the drive into the mountains to the rebel stronghold of Perquín.

Chapter Seventeen

An Emerging *Directiva*

"Through the twelve years of war there's been the forced captures of civilians and the military roadblocks that didn't allow food and medicines or other goods to pass through up into this zone. But nonetheless, despite all these obstacles, we have been able to continue to move forward to build."

Early the next morning, it was still dark when I was awakened by the sounds of splashing water next to my head. I was confused. It sounded like a waterfall outside the bunk house. It took a few moments for me to realize that men were dumping cans of water on themselves in the shower stalls, sending the contents cascading to the floor.

With all the noise, sleep was impossible, so I got up and looked out the open front door. The sun wasn't up and a heavy fog covered the road in front of the dorm, partially obscuring the shacks beyond. Across the way, shrouded in mist, a line of men, dressed in work clothes with straw sombreros on their heads and machetes at their sides, ambled down toward the macadam road to an awaiting bus.

Fully awake, and the splashing water stopped by now, I grabbed my towel and walked around to the back of the bunkhouse to check out the showers for myself. The three stalls were empty. In the first stall, I undressed, placed my clothes and towel on a hook, dipped the ladling can in the drum of water, stood a moment with my bare feet on the flat stones, took a deep breath, then dumped the cold water on my head.

— 2 —

By 6:30 we had assembled in front of the dorms, then followed Sinclair a short distance to a building set back from the road. Inside men ate breakfast at long wooden tables. We sat at one of the tables and a woman from the kitchen poured us coffees. Then from a large pot she ladled out beans and rice on paper plates and placed them in front of us.

Groaning about a lack of sleep, we poked at the food. Torriera, not feeling well this morning, was doing her best to keep up appearances, while Reid and Willison, over their bouts with stomach cramps, ate with gusto.

"How much rape and incest is there in this country?" Ventura asked Sinclair.

"There is a good deal of it," Sinclair replied. "Both in the homes and in the streets."

Ventura thought for a moment. "There is need of a good sociological study of the people of this country," he said. "Is there one?"

Sinclair looked up from his coffee. "Segundo Montes." Then he outlined the schedule for the morning. "We'll walk back to the dorm, get our gear in order, and drive up to the pavilion to interview a spokesperson from the cooperative. After a tour of Segundo Montes, we'll have lunch, then drive to Perquín."

Back at the dorms it was too early for the morning interview, so Willison and I walked across a field to where the land dropped off. Cloud formations obscured much of the valley in the distance, but closer to where we stood was a field of corn and below a stream flashed in the sun.

"I'm going to explore this path and see if I can get some photos," said Willison, who besides being an experienced world trekker and avid sportsman, turned out to be a serious amateur photographer. I circled back to check out the community *baño.*

Opening the door and peering inside, I decided to wait for the bathrooms at the pavilion, wondering who if anyone was responsible for cleaning up the soiled newspapers littering the dirt floor. With dysentery and diarrhea rampant in the country, wouldn't the leadership council be on top of the situation? Whoever was in charge, it wasn't happening.

— 3 —

The morning meeting was scheduled for around 8 o'clock, and we drove past the open air market, the community bank, a few scattered buildings, then turned back up the hill. In one clearing several people waited their turns to draw water from a well, and off to the side a young woman stood over a pail washing her upper body. The scene reminded me of a Gauguin painting.

The top of the hill was drenched in sunlight, and the air was heavy and sweet. We left the vans, skirted around puddles from the rain the night before, and sat in the pavilion, filling three picnic tables pushed together with notepads, pens, water bottles, cameras, and tape recorders.

A representative from the cooperative, a young woman, possibly in her late twenties, with broad cheekbones and dark hair falling to her shoulders, sat next to Sinclair. The tape recorders made her nervous, and she asked Sinclair why they were there.

Sinclair translated her question, and Reid responded, "For my students in my classes."

That assured her enough to allow the recorders to be turned on.

Testimony of the Segundo Montes
"Public Relations" Representative

I want to give you a very warm reception here at the community of Segundo Montes. For us, it is very important to have visiting groups because it has been our consolation through the years to have international visitors. It might be helpful for you to understand a little bit of our history, why we left El Salvador, and what our life was like in the Colomoncagua refugee camp in Honduras.

In 1979-1980 a civil war is unleashed. The attempt was, more than anything, to destroy the rural areas, such as Morazán and Chalatenango. The situation was intolerable, and people couldn't survive here. We were obliged to leave the country and go to our neighboring country of Honduras.

The first group fled from here on December l3, 1980. The second group fled December 14, 1980. The first group was four hundred and fifty people who fled. The second group was six hundred people. We got to Colomoncagua, and that's where we began to live again. The Catholic Church received us, and the *campesino* communities received us. However we were received very poorly by the Honduran Army and the Honduran government.

In December of 1981, the Salvadoran Army undertook a military operation, massacring about a thousand *campesinos* in the town of El Mozote in the province of Morazán. This forced more and more people to flee into Honduras. From 1981 to 1984, the population within the refugee camp grew to eight thousand four hundred people.

Life in the refugee camp was very difficult. It was costly. It cost our blood, our lives, and people were killed there. This obligated us to become more united, to make greater efforts to resist the repression of the Honduran Army. In some ways, life in the refugee camps over those nine years gave us a lot of advantages. In other ways it was very costly. Some of the advantages were that we were able to educate ourselves. We went from a population which was largely illiterate farmers to people who had vocational training.

Because of the need for unity we created an organization that was very vertical in terms of leadership. Decisions were made at the top and transmitted to the bottom. There was no circulation of money in the refugee camp. Everyone worked in exchange for the assistance they received. The United Nations High Commission for

Refugees gave us assistance so we could live, and the different agencies gave us training in different skills. Thanks to this, this is what the future will be for us here in El Salvador.

We had always said we wanted to return to our country when there was peace. We stayed very tuned in to what was happening here in our country. As Salvadorans, it is really not in our nature to remain on the outside as spectators. We looked for ways to insert ourselves. After looking at different changes, such as President Arias of Costa Rica's initiative to bring peace to the region, and then things such as the Conference for Refugees in Guatemala, we made the decision to return. Those kinds of reforms were looking towards the future of peace in Central America.

During the Conference of Refugees meetings, we elaborated our proposal to return, and sent it to that meeting. Then we began negotiations and discussions with the Salvadoran Government to discuss the conditions upon which we would return. We reached an agreement to return to our country on November 9, 1989, but because of the offensive we couldn't go on that date.

Since we had been preparing for the return for two months and we had all packed our goods, the people were disappointed that we couldn't go back. So those who had the greatest courage decided to return on November 18, walking during the middle of the offensive. On December 9, another group left from the camp to go home, also walking. We got right up here to the top of the hill where we are standing, and that's where we stayed, working, settling the land. It was very hard for those two months.

Then from January 14, the returns were much more negotiated, based on a tripartite agreement between the United Nations High Commission for Refugees, the Honduran and Salvadoran Governments, and the refugees. It is probably necessary to add that during the first two repatriations there was no support from any international organization. During the subsequent repatriations, there was support.

Returning to your country is really hard, but now with the support of the international community, people made the effort to make it happen. We are not talking about things being costly or requiring a lot of work. What I mean is that through the twelve years of war there's been the forced captures of civilians, and the military roadblocks that didn't allow food and medicines or other goods to pass through up into this zone. But nonetheless, despite all these obstacles, we have been able to continue to move forward to build.

When we got here there were eight thousand five hundred people divided among five different settlements. There was a need for organization, a new treaty organization, to adapt each year to the changes. One of the things we arrived at in terms of organization was an assembly which sets up broad guidelines for the direction of the community. The assembly is made up of two representatives for every two hundred people in the community. In addition to these two representatives of every organized sector, there are other projects. The assembly consists of about three hundred people, and that is the highest decision-making group in the community.

Initially this group was set up to meet every six months, but we've been meeting every three months. It is this group that names the leadership committee by a secret ballot. The leadership committee, the *directiva*, is named for a two-year period. Their function is to discuss and define the implementation of each of the projects. The *directiva* is made up of thirteen people, including myself. And ten of the thirteen who make up the *directiva* are also the heads of separate organizations here.

And if Colomancagua could be characterized as decision-making from top to bottom, here decision-making is always from the bottom, giving orders and directives to the top. The social organization is separated from the productive organizations. Anything that has to do with services is in the social group. The business group is in charge of both production and marketing. The finance group is the bank. Then there is a development or fund-raising group, which has to do with administration, relations, and project writing.

In the first two years of our work here, I think we were trying to reproduce the model of direction which we experienced in Colomoncagua as community organizations. But in reality there's been some very significant changes in our model. In Colomoncagua, it was training. Here it has to be producing. We've been doing feasibility studies here on how to increase the efficiency of work, of productivity. If you had known our work previously, and then when you see the projects we have now, you'll see the differences. For example, there is the hen project, or the egg laying project, which actually brings in a lot of income for the community. The brick making factory. The metal works, making pots and pans and things, and also factories for shoes and clothing. And ninety head of cattle which give milk. We really are interested in increases in productivity and efficiency because the money or the salaries that people earn are based on those incomes. Currently we've finished the stage of provisional housing, and we're beginning to build permanent housing. The education project is pretty much in place. The health work has many more limitations, but we are making progress and doing what we can in that area. Of all the services, those are sustained by the community here.

The government has not apportioned the assistance it should in any community. So our efforts are in the direction of how can we reach agreements with the government so they cover the services which are their obligation. It's as if the crises and emergencies really never end, and we are working on a permanent basis fulltime.

— 4 —

"Maybe that could be a brief background," Sinclair said. "We'd like to ask some questions."

Q) Could she say a little bit about the development of this political structure from something that is very vertical? She said that when they were in the refugee camp and even when they were first here it was very vertical, and then they had something that was very democratic. Could she talk a little a bit about how that more democratic structure developed?

A) It was a different situation in Colomancagua. And it required a different model. We were surrounded by the military, we couldn't leave, there was no money, and there were the needs for a lot of unity and efficiency in our life there. Basically all our problems were resolved by Agency money. Our communities here have been based on the needs to be able to do marketing, to be able to operate in a free country, to operate where there's no openings, and the need to change.

What we need to do is to strengthen and give impulse to participatory democracy because without that there is nothing here. And also we don't want to be a closed community. We want to be open and to be seen well by the rest of society and the surrounding communities. It is necessary that we integrate into other communities in a good way. Nor do we want to be an isolated community that has more privileges and more assistance.

Q) When the directors are named, is that based on the recommendations by the people, or do they campaign?

A) They are elected by secret ballot. Two hundred people have a meeting, and they are the ones who elect the two representatives.

Q) Tell us how it was they were able to stay here when they came, and why they were not displaced by the government or others.

A) When we came it was in the midst of the big offensive. But most of the fighting was in the capital and not here in the countryside. We could defend ourselves by staying in the community. We were large enough to protect ourselves through community organization.

"Just as an example," said Sinclair, "I was in the camps when they came back, and one of the things they brought back were these two wooden tablets. And I asked them what they were, because I wasn't quite sure. They said they were windows or doors. And after a while they showed me. It was a little printing press. They had block letters carved out of wood which they could line in there. It was like a little mimeograph, and they could print out human rights violations. If they were to be attacked, they could print a thousand of these things and distribute them everywhere. It shows what community organization can do."

Q) Are teachers paid by the government?

A) The government doesn't pay the salaries of the teachers. There are some volunteers, as well as some agencies paying those salaries. When we returned from Colomoncagua, we had international volunteers giving training to the teachers. There are one hundred and forty teachers for a student population of a fraction over two thousand students from kindergarten to sixth grade.

Q) What about social organizations with certain services? What would the services be in those social organizations?

A) Health, education, social communication, the community organizations, urban development, and public relations. And I represent the relations.

Q) Could she talk a bit more about economic models? Whether the workers in the shoe factory are paid an hourly wage?

A) When we speak about alternative models, we really refer to alternative models for ourselves and not necessarily for other parts of the country, because here we really don't have a high degree of training or skills, so we do it as a program for us but not necessarily for others. And the land up here in Morazán is not that fertile, so the only alternative is to strengthen efforts like the clothing factory.

There are different salary levels according to people's responsibilities. The salary for workers, for most of the people, would be about three hundred and fifty colones. About forty-three dollars a month. Very low salaries. But the agencies don't give any monies for salaries. What we pay salaries with is from the goods that we produce and sell.

It's a real struggle because the process of developing this alternative takes years. It's not something that happens in a day. We lived with a refugee mentality for ten years, which was ten years of receiving. We understand that we are probably a little backward in that sense. It is not easy to leave behind some of the attitudes that the people had.

Q) What about the assembly election process?

A) Everyone in this assembly has to be named from the group they represent. And if there is an absence, the General Assembly cannot name someone else to substitute for them.

Q) Do the people who become directors make it known that they want to serve as directors, or are they called upon by the others in the assembly to serve?

A) Let me give you an example. We are all members of the assembly. Within this group we all know each other, and we can nominate someone in this group to be voted on. Since we are all members of the assembly, any of us is qualified. Anyone who others judge to be qualified and capable and interested in doing it would be elected. Thirty people are nominated. And out of the thirty nominated, thirteen people are elected.

Q) How is the leadership set up?

A) The leadership would have a coordinator, an assistant coordinator, and a treasurer, and the others would represent the different areas.

Q) Is there any problem about documentation? I'm thinking of the voting in 1994 and so on. Is there a problem?

A) Only two thousand people, all under ten years of age, have the appropriate documentation, like a birth certificate from El Salvador. The rest of the adults, there will be one hundred people who have Salvadoran identification.

Q) Does this cause a problem then if they want to vote?

A) It's a concern for us. The government has had two laws which call for the documentation and voter registration, and as soon as they are published in the official government journals, then we'll move forward in looking for other documentation.

Q) My understanding is that the government wanted to put all kinds of services up here. Why is that not happening, and what kinds of services do they want from the government?

A) In terms of education, the government really hasn't made any efforts. They just talk. In health there seems to be more interest, but we question how much is interest and how much is propaganda. In terms of electrification, yes there are plans. It's part of the national reconstruction plan, but we are in the third stage of that, which would be the fifth year, so there's nothing imminent. In terms of water there are no government plans. Roads? They have been building some roads up here, although it's not too much. In regards to telephones, it's really that things happen bilaterally. We'll go speak with a particular department in this region or in this department capital and try and work things out. But in terms of a central government role in helping us with services, there's been no negotiations or discussions.

Q) In the "returns" that she talked about, she said they had the means to defend themselves. Does this mean they were totally non-violent? Were they prepared non-violently, or were they prepared militarily?

A) Non-violent.

Q) Could she just briefly describe what health services they have, and what the government has stated they might help with?

A) In the refugee camp in Colomoncagua, there was a group of health promoters and health personnel who were trained within our population. Doctors Without Borders supported our work in the refugee camp and are supporting our work here. There are about two thousand consultations that happen on a monthly basis. Ten percent of them are referred to Doctors Without Borders. We've received outside assistance to buy medicines, and also Doctors Without Borders have been supplying some medicines. It's not as if the government has offered or come here, but we have sought them to begin these negotiations. We were very insistent with them for their involvement, and they did come here, and they did a survey of what our needs are, and there have been no concrete results from that. What they have done is a vaccination campaign, but anything beyond that has not happened.

Q) How much assistance is coming in?

A) There are different figures on how much assistance we have because it comes from different agencies. Just the European community would be the housing program that comes to about a total of a million colones, or about one hundred and fifty thousand dollars. Within some of the productive enterprises, the investments have been about five hundred thousand colones, or sixty thousand dollars. More generally, because I don't think I have the figures for each area, all the work we have done here has been through outside assistance. And it's not been through any governmental help. It's been through international assistance and solidarity.

Q) Is it up to the government to administer outside funds and deliver services?

A) It's been our experience that the government's use of funding has been handled very poorly. We have funding for a two-year period. I'm not sure when it started, but it ends halfway through next year. But in terms of answering your question, we feel the government really has a responsibility to cover the social services, health and education particularly. In regards to assistance for the productive enterprises and the community work, I think that should go directly to the community. The government has always looked at this very suspiciously, even as belonging to the FMLN, so I don't think it would be good for them to handle that money.

On other kinds of projects such as health and education, we're not really sure where the Ministry of Education is. We've asked them for letters of support, and sometimes we get it, and sometimes we don't. It's a very shadowy kind of situation. It's hard for us to make decisions when there's no clarity. And there's also a difference, I think, between the response of involvement with basic healthcare here for the community, but they shouldn't be involved in our work to become more productive.

Q) Relative to the social control, relative to violations, meaning thefts, violence, or general uncooperativeness with the collective conscience or the agreements of a particular society, what type of social control would they have for these violations?

A) In terms of those who do not want to be part of the collective conscience or the collective work, they can follow their own individual work, do a little bit of farming, or put up their own individual stores, and there's no problem. There's another group that is also dedicated to more individual initiatives, and that is because the amount of work in the collective is not big enough to keep everyone productive. But to the degree that people work together or on their own is up to the people. There is space for everybody.

Since the cease-fire, there has been a growing social decomposition here, a slipping way. There's been more drinking, a little bit more theft, more street disturbances. It's a large job to keep the public order here. If someone beats someone up, for example, and draws blood, that person will be arrested for seventy-two hours, and the victim, through a process, will be indemnified by the offender.

In anything that's more extreme, such as a death, there is a crew that investigates it here, and takes the information to the local judge and the judge would assess the information and decide if there is enough evidence to warrant issuing an arrest. In other cases, such as a young person who steals something, after we've done an investigation, there will be a meeting with the young person, and if he or she recognizes and accepts responsibility for the actions, there will be a general meeting, and the young person has to make a confession in front of the whole community. These are the different procedures we have to correct any kind of problems that come up.

The story of the people of Segundo Montes echoed much of what we had already heard at Tierra Blanca, Hacienda California, and Nueva Esperanza: the urgent need when the civil war broke out to flee the country to safety, the brutality of the Salvadoran Army and its "scorched earth" policies, the mixed blessings of years spent as refugees in a neighboring country, the desire to return to their native land to rebuild their lives, and finally what transpired when they arrived on Salvadoran soil with little more than the clothes on their backs.

The spokesperson's job was to paint a positive picture, but even if only half of what she said was true, Segundo Montes was a successful collective. They had managed to eke out a subsistence living with the support of the international community, had developed their own structure of democratic governance, and at the same time they were working on projects that would allow for future self-sufficiency.

Our plan, for the rest of the morning, was to visit several of those projects.

Chapter Eighteen

The Best Shop in the Mountains

"Our workers have little or no technical training, so we learn from experience. Only two of the workers have any kind of specialized training. So we read about what we are supposed to do, and we learn from the problems that we have overcome."

At our first stop, a leather and weaving shop, several women sat at tables, cutting and sewing, surrounded by piles of discarded leather on the floor. One young woman, hunched over a 4x8 foot plywood table, her long hair pulled back and tied with a ribbon, cut the soles of sandals, first tracing the outline of a sole from a pattern, then following the outline by pressing down on the thick leather with the sharpened point of a foot-long knife. Next, the sole in her hand, she trimmed off the excess leather, stopping from time to time to sharpen the blade's cutting edge.

In a cavernous room to the rear of the leather shop weavers scrambled back and forth in front of looms interlacing strands of blue, yellow, red, and orange plastic rope into hammocks, their hands a blur, they worked so fast. One young man in dungarees and a blue work shirt, sleeves rolled to his elbows, walked along a stretched out hammock with a fist full of yellow strands in his right hand, weaving the plastic into the next layer. In back a woman sat on the floor attaching ropes from the ends of the finished hammocks to steel rings. A skilled person, we were told, could finish one hammock, selling for 120 colones or roughly $15, in about four days.

Next we visited the leather goods store overflowing with handbags, belts, riding chaps, and ornate scabbards for machetes. We hadn't purchased machetes yet, so the scabbards could wait, but a colorful hammock would make a fine addition to the yard back home. The woman in charge of the store sat behind a desk, and when asked if she had any for sale pointed to a table in the back piled high with hammocks in different sizes. The right size was no problem, but packing the bulky item for the return trip to Connecticut would be a hassle. Our plan was to donate clothes we didn't need when leaving the country, but even minus the shirts and dungarees left behind, I wasn't sure I could stuff the hammock into my suitcase. But a genuine Salvadoran hammock for $12? I bought one.

Outside the shop, Willison and Romeo, full of energy and laughing like two kids, chased each other between the parked vehicles. Then Willison stopped and made believe he was a fly fisherman, casting an imaginary rod to hook and reel in the last person in our group lingering in the leather store. At least he and Romeo felt chipper, which could not be said for several of the rest us fighting stomach cramps becoming more persistent as the morning progressed.

We retraced the way we came, turned right, and pulled up in front of an electric generating facility and behind it a large open-sided carpentry shop, where the high whine of a rip saw and the smell of freshly-cut wood filled the air. Inside, men worked with table saws, lathes, and assorted wood-working tools assembling desks, tables, bureaus, chairs, and coffins.

One worker was fitting the last board to the top of a bureau. The plank, about five feet long, was too wide by roughly an inch, and rather than rip off the extra inch of wood with a table saw, he stood the board on end, eyed it, and hacked a series of cuts with his machete about an inch apart down one side. Next, with the machete, he sliced away the hacked wood, turned the board on its side, and ran a plane over the cut edge. Finally he sighted along the new edge of the board, and satisfied with the result, replaced it on top of the bureau. A perfect fit.

At our next stop, a clothing factory, women bent over industrial sewing machines on tables covered with heaps of yellow and red fabric and spools of thread. A fashion show was scheduled for that afternoon, and teenage girls were laughing and milling around trying on skirts and dresses and practicing to walk like runway models.

To the rear of the shoe factory, shelves lining the walls were crammed with shoes, sandals, and boots.

"We're struggling to fill an order for four thousand new boots," the man in charge said. "The order which is much larger than usual, was accepted so we could move to a higher level of competition. So now everyone is working extra hours to meet our deadline, and we're not sure if we can finish the order on time."

He looked stressed, but the workers were churning out boots as if their lives depended on filling that order.

—— 2 ——

The next to last stop for the morning was the Segundo Montes Bank. At the bottom of the hill under trees in front of the bank an open air market was in session, its tables filled with hats, shirts, dresses, and trinkets. We walked past the tables and around the back to a small office to listen to a presentation by Gloria, coordinator of the community bank's Loan Department.

Testimony of Bank Officer

> The bank was one of the first things set up in Segundo Montes. Refugees were awarded some money when they were repatriated, so we asked the people to deposit their money here in the bank, rather than spend it all. Ninety-five percent of the people agreed to deposit their money, and we offer ten percent interest, paid at the end of the year.

Our workers have little or no technical training, so we learn from experience. Only two of the workers have any kind of specialized training. So we read about what we are supposed to do, and we learn from the problems that we have overcome.

Q) How much money was given to the refugees when they returned to El Salvador?

A) About three hundred and twenty colones for each adult, and one hundred and sixty colones for each child under sixteen. Because the first groups to arrive here did not return under the normal repatriation procedures, they did not receive any monies, so the community shared money with them. The adults in the community gave fifty-eight colones each to the members of the first and second groups.

Q) How does the bank decide on giving loans to people?

A) We evaluate the creditors based on their health, moral virtues, and their ability to repay the loan. Also the person must allow the bank to supervise the project that the money was borrowed for.

The government has not imposed any conditions on our bank, but it hasn't offered any help either. We are considered an internal group, rather than a legal organization. But to our credit, we have not made any loans that have not been fully paid back. Generally we work with the people to work out any problems.

Q) What is the net worth of the bank?

A) About half a million colones [roughly $62,500].

Their work ethic reminded me of what Sr. Elena had said when talking about the lack of doctors and the need for health care and medicines in her community. They read books, planted medicinal herbs, and taught themselves. In this case, the unofficial bank of Segundo Montes paid ten percent on deposits, with every loan fully repaid with no government supervision.

Next we stopped at a pre-school cooperative in a building surrounded by a six foot wire fence with a large mural on an outside side wall depicting the slain Jesuit Father Montes surrounded by young children. The teachers turned our visit into a celebration, explaining to their charges that we were visitors from the United States, and would they show us we were welcome. With that, the children laughed and clapped and joined in singing us a song.

All in all, the community representative's story about Segundo Montes, shared with us earlier at the pavilion, proved true. The place hummed with activity.

— 3 —

As we stood in front of the open-air market, Sacco was surprised to see Deimas, the war-wounded guerrilla he had met at the plaza in San Salvador on Wednesday night. Deimas recognized Sacco immediately, smiled from ear to ear, embracing him like an old friend.

"We have to get a picture of this," said Sacco, delighted to find Deimas again. "We promised each other we'd look for one another when we got to Segundo Montes."

"Stand next to the road," I said, "and I'll take a picture."

Deimas, wearing Sacco's NYPD cap and standing straight in spite of his leg operation, lined up next to his beaming friend, both talking excitedly in Spanish, trying to make out what the other was saying. I asked McAllister what was going on.

"Deimas is saying that he is in Segundo Montes to help the cooperative any way he can."

It was all we could do to drag Sacco away from his new compatriot when it was time to return to the pavilion to discuss plans for the afternoon trip to Perquín.

"I need to see if I can find a straw hat," Wickwire said to me. "I'm just going to look in this outdoor market and I'll join you later."

"Is it alright if I stay here with Chester?" I asked Sinclair. "He wants to look over the items on the tables."

"It's a good idea," he said. "But stay together."

With that, the others drove up the hill toward the administration pavilion, and the two of us turned toward the market.

Against a pile of multi-colored plastic jugs, a yellow sign, translated from Spanish read, "The best shop in the mountains with the lowest prices."

The first table held stacks of straw hats. Wickwire leaned his canes against the side of the table and started trying on one hat after another.

"I can't find one that fits," he said, laughing. "My head is too big."

Anxious for a sale, the woman rummaged through the stacks, intent on finding one that fit. She'd select one, hand it to Wickwire, and he'd try it on. Then she'd grab another one and hand it over. All were too small.

"I'll buy one of these caps," Wickwire said finally, pointing at the caps with adjustable plastic bands in the back. "I really don't need it," he confided, "but I'll buy it anyway."

"Why?" I asked. "If you don't need it, why buy it?"

"These people have so little," he said. "It doesn't cost that much, and it's very important that they make a sale."

Balancing on his two canes, he pulled out his wallet and paid for the cap. "This will make a good present," he added, smiling at the woman.

Stones and roots covered the ground by the tables, and I worried about him tripping, but he didn't hesitate for a moment, walking slowly, picking his way through the market.

"I need to find something for my wife," I said.

That's all Wickwire needed to hear. He walked over to a woman sitting at a nearby table, explained I was looking for a present for my wife, and she immediately got up, collected an assortment of shirts and dresses, then dropped the heap on the table in front of me. As I flipped through the clothes, looking for something that might catch my eye, the woman stood next to me, waiting expectantly.

"The idea is to buy something, anything," he said. "I don't like to spend their time and not make some small purchase."

When I couldn't make up my mind, Wickwire picked up what looked like a toy purse, handed it to the woman, and paid for it.

— 4 —

The sky was beginning to cloud over when we arrived shortly after noon at the administration area on top of the hill. In the pavilion two cameramen were busy videotaping a meeting of men and women seated at the picnic tables.

"It's an FMLN meeting," Wickwire said.

A white station wagon with the words "*Naciones Unidad*" [United Nations] under the side windows pulled up and two women got out and walked toward the pavilion.

"That is Ana Guadalupe Martinez," Wickwire whispered, motioning to one of them, a short, round-faced woman dressed in faded jeans, a large white T-shirt, and white sneakers. At the time her name meant nothing to me.

Martinez smiled when she recognized Wickwire, they greeted each other, then moved off to a table to talk in private. At one point I overheard Wickwire say, "We are in solidarity in total."

The other woman, who wore combat boots, green pants, and a white shirt, and looked to be in her late teens or early twenties, joined the on-going conversations at the tables. I could not stop looking at her. She was beautiful.

Later I asked Wickwire, "Who is Ana Guadalupe Martinez?"

"She is a famous guerrilla commander," he said, "a member of the central command of the Farabundo Martí National Liberation Front, and the author of the book *Clandestine Cells.* She wrote about her experiences when captured by the Salvadoran Army, and it is one of the most important books to come out of the war. Ana Martinez surfaced after the cease fire and became one of the chief negotiators of the rebel leaders for the peace plan."

"Would you mind me asking what you were talking to her about?"

"We were talking about the National University, and I was asking her why Fabio Castillio doesn't have the support of many of the professors. You have to understand that the FMLN think of the university as their alma mater. Also she feels that Christiani is the one who is blocking the money. She said that she is still concerned about the legal system and getting it implemented. And then there are the problems with the National Guard and the Hacienda Police. Basically, a lot of things that should be happening under the peace accords are not, as far as she is concerned."

With the FMLN group deep in conversation, we sat at separate tables, ate lunch, and Sinclair explained the possibilities for our afternoon trip to Perquín.

"There are two places we could visit," he said. "The first was a guerrilla stronghold during the war, and the other is a village that managed to survive the war intact. The second place sells native goods. Also two women will be accompanying us to Perquín."

Did he mean Ana Martinez and the young woman? I hoped so.

"I haven't been able to visit these areas before, but now since the peace accords are in effect it's relatively safe to travel there."

He paused looking around the table. "So how many of you are in favor of visiting the guerrilla stronghold?"

Several of us raised our hands.

"How about the village and its market?"

Again we raised our hands.

At that point the overhead clouds opened up and sheets of rain pelted the tile roof.

"This would be a good time for all of you to spend some unstructured time by yourselves," Sinclair said. "Some spiritual time to try put things into some kind of perspective."

— 5 —

With that in mind and the rain taking the edge off the midday heat, some of us drifted off to write in journals while others sat and talked over the possibilities for afternoon's trip.

Meanwhile the young guerrilla with Martinez was looking at Willison.

"She's checking you out."

Then Reid walked over to where I was sitting. "Ralph, I need to talk to you," he said, motioning me to follow him to another table.

"What would you think about not going to Perquín this afternoon?"

"What are you talking about?"

"It seems some of the women are not so sure that going to Perquín is a good idea. They would rather go back to the hotel in San Salvador."

"What did you say?"

"Some of the women would rather go back to the hotel in San Salvador."

"Why?"

"They don't feel well enough to make the trip, so I'm just taking an informal survey of the group to see how people feel about the afternoon. Did you want to go to Perquín?"

"That's what we came here for. Yes, I want to go very much."

"I'll have to talk to the others to see what they think."

Called together, we sat in a circle on the left side of the pavilion away from the FMLN meeting, and just as we sat down, two young boys grabbed Wickwire's crutches and ran off with them. Pretending they had broken legs, they hobbled around on the crutches, laughing and having a grand time.

"That's really not a good idea," Wickwire said, worried they might hurt themselves.

The children did not want to give up the crutches, but finally were told they had to stop.

"Several people have voiced reservations about traveling to Perquín this afternoon," said Reid, addressing the group. "I thought it would be a good idea to come together to discuss the issues, to see if we could arrive at a consensus about what to do. Why don't we go around the circle and give each person a chance to speak. Then we can take a vote if necessary."

"You mean as soon as anyone gets dirt under their fingernails, we have to turn back?" someone asked.

"This is ridiculous," said another. "We all knew what we were getting into. We knew this wasn't going to be an easy trip. We're feeling sick too, but we still want to see Perquín."

No one had slept well. And several of us suffered from stomach cramps and frayed nerves. But the men, except Ventura, wanted to continue. Bertsch remained undecided. The rest of the women favored returning to San Salvador, saying we would not be seeing anything new in Perquín.

"We have two vans," I said, hoping a compromise might be worked out. "If some people want to return to the hotel, why can't they go back, and the rest of us take the other van to Perquín?"

"That's not possible," Sinclair said. "We are a group, and we can't split up. It's not good for the group, and it's not safe."

As much as anyone, Sinclair had been looking forward to visiting Perquín, but under the circumstances we had to turn back.

"Ok," he said. "We'll leave shortly as soon as I explain to our hosts that we've decided not to travel to Perquín, and that we'll not be staying over another night."

Hoping to salvage the group spirit, Sinclair said he could arrange a visit to the San Salvador bazaar the next day, an enormous market where everything imaginable was for sale.

But even with Sinclair's suggestion in mind, we left the pavilion walking toward the vans, the women in one group, the men in the other, avoiding talking. Group cohesion was in tatters.

"How do you feel about not going to Perquín?" I asked Willison.

"I don't want to talk about it," he snapped.

In the parking area the young woman accompanying Ana Martinez was standing by the driver's side of our van, asking when we were leaving for Perquín. When told our plans had changed, she looked disappointed.

Meanwhile, a photographer was taking pictures of Martinez and a guerrilla *compadre* in camouflage fatigues and combat boots. Both stood next to the white *Naciones Unidas* vehicle, smiling. I thought Martinez looked happy and healthy, and not at all what a war-torn guerrilla commander might be expected to look like.

— 6 —

Back at the dorm, I managed to create my own ruckus when I walked over to my pack under the cot by the door, knelt down, unzippered the top, and started rearranging my clothes.

"Yaaaiii!" I screamed.

"What are you yelling about?" Sacco asked. Reid and McAllister looked at me like I was nuts.

"My hands! They're on fire!"

I didn't know what was happening. I held them to my face, expecting to see reddish blotches. I saw nothing. I looked closer. Then I saw them. Ants. So tiny they were almost invisible. Scurrying all over my hands.

"Fire ants!" I yelled.

I started shaking my hands to get rid of them, but the burning continued. I peered into my pack. Ants were swarming around in the clothes. I ran out the door, rubbing and shaking my hands until the burning dissipated.

Returning inside, I grabbed each article of clothing, raced back out the door and shook it outside. Back inside, I left the clothing on top of the cot, then grabbed the next piece. Finally, with the pack empty, I shook it outside as well, thinking I'd have to recheck the clothing at the hotel.

"You left your pack open," commented Sinclair. "Did you have any food in there?"

"Some cheese and snack bars."

"That's what attracted them."

Chapter Nineteen

The Pastoral Lourdes Retreat House

"It's the spirit of the Salvadorans. They know how to survive with hope. It's an issue of faith that lives and breathes in the face of every kind of devastation."

When we started the drive back to San Salvador, the women in one van, the men in the other, the topic of Perquín was off limits. But by the time we reached the gas station where we stopped for sodas the day before, it had dawned on all of us that returning to the Alameda Hotel meant a good night's sleep and a free morning before meeting for our wrap-up session.

Later that night we sat at a long table in a Chinese restaurant with Sinclair working on the schedule for the next afternoon. "We'll need a planning committee to structure the meeting," he said. "It's important. It'll give everybody a chance to come together one last time for reflection and sharing. You need time to put the whole trip into some kind of perspective. And you need to make plans for what will happen when you arrived back in the States."

— 2 —

The next morning, the bazaar, an enormous in-door complex covering a city block, turned out to be a madhouse of frenetic activity with shopkeepers calling out to bargain hunters jamming the aisles between stalls, booths, and tables laden with leather shoes, boots, belts, handbags, piles of shirts, dresses, pants, jackets, coats, straw hats, pins, buckles, tote bags, machetes, knives, beads, watches, and all kinds of souvenirs.

In stall after stall, vendors gestured for passersby to look at their goods, promising the best prices. If you stopped, the vendor would smile broadly, walk over and touch your arm, and beckon you to enter.

Sinclair had warned us that prices were to be considered starting points. Haggling was expected. The final price depended on how much the buyer wanted the item and was willing to pay. Prices for the same item, guaranteed always as "the lowest available," could be purchased, you discovered, for considerably less in another shop an aisle or two away.

One table was piled high with leather goods, and an old woman dressed head to toe in black, picked up a belt, motioning for me to hold it.

"*Quánto cuesta*?" ["How much?"]

The woman muttered a price and added a comment.

"She says one hundred and thirty colones," said Sacco, "and how wonderful the belt is."

I said I did not need so fine a belt.

The woman placed the belt in my hands. It was an alligator belt.

"No," I said, handing it back.

"How much did I want to pay for the belt?" she asked.

"No," I said again, feeling guilty.

She begged me to reconsider.

I walked away, Wickwire's comment about the importance of purchasing items from vendors again ringing in my ears.

At one point Barker walked by sporting a smart-looking multi-colored jacket draped over her arm.

"That looks like a work of art," I said.

"A present to myself," she announced, smiling. "I know it's a lot of money, but I really like it."

Later, back from Mass, a beaming Torreira joined us carrying four machetes, the blades pointing in different directions. "I'll hide them in my luggage," she said, laughing.

"I need to look for a pair of shoes," said Sacco. "I can't pass up these bargains. I could never buy anything at home for these prices."

Outside the bazaar, we crossed the street to another block of stalls where Sacco purchased a straw hat. After setting the brim at a rakish angle, with his gray mustache, tanned skin, and wearing sun glasses, I had to admit, he cut a dashing figure.

"I want to go to the police headquarters," he announced.

"I've read too much about Central America," Gradie commented. "I'm not going anywhere near a police station."

"What do you mean?" I asked.

"I just don't think you can ever trust them. So if you're going, just be careful."

Her comment reminded me of the sketches I'd seen of prisoners hung upside down with ropes, legs spread, beaten bloody and senseless in underground dungeons.

"Do you mind if we go?" Sacco asked.

"Go ahead," she said. "I'm returning to the hotel."

I was certain we were asking for trouble. But already Sacco was leaning into the open window of a parked cab, asking for directions, and the cabbie pointed down the street.

We waved goodbye to our group and started walking. And I'm thinking, this is crazy.

"You're too apprehensive," he said. "We'll be fine."

Soon we came to a park surrounded by walls where a National Police guard in pressed olive army fatigues was talking to a young woman. Sacco asked him for directions to the police station, and the guard, impatient with the interruption, waved us down the street.

— 3 —

The station, where men in uniforms lounged under trees while others bustled in and out the front door, was a massive stone fortress-like building complete with barred windows. It occupied an entire city block, its front protected by concrete barriers.

Sacco approached a guard to explain about the caps and how he hoped to make some trades. The officer seemed to understand and motioned us toward the front door.

At the door another officer stopped us, asking what we wanted. Sacco pulled out his wallet, flashed his New York *"Teniente"* [Lieutenant] badge, then held out his NYPD caps and again tried to explain his mission. The officer nodded and held open the door.

Inside the cavernous lobby, spinning off in different directions, were stone hallways which I imagined led to subterranean cells where tortured FMLN insurgents rotted away. To our left two officers sat behind desks. One was slightly heavy, clean shaven, and looked to be in his thirties; the other was an older powerfully-built man with three gold bars on his shoulder.

"He's probably a major and the platoon commander," Sacco whispered. "The man in charge."

He stared at us.

"*Soy de la policía de Nueva York, pero estoy retirado ahora.*" ["I was in the New York police, but I've retired now."]

The two officers looked at him and said nothing. Quickly Sacco pulled out his wallet, again flipped to his NYPD Lieutenant badge, and held it toward the officers.

"Fui teniente y ahora mi hijo es policía en Nueva York. El quiere cambiar este sombrero y patches por suyos." ["I was a lieutenant, and my son is a policeman in New York, and he wants to exchange this hat and patches for yours."]

The older one scowled.

"Si, comprendo. Esperate" ["Wait a second. I understand"], the other said, and called over an orderly, spoke to him, and the orderly walked off.

"I told him to check upstairs for patches or caps to be exchanged," the officer said in English.

Meanwhile the officer in command turned back to his paper work, acting as if we were an unwanted distraction. His face appeared menacing, and as I stood in front of the desk I had the uncanny feeling that this man was capable of torturing and killing prisoners, and had more than likely done so.

While I'm standing there thinking these thoughts, the orderly returned. We would be taken to where the caps and patches could be swapped. The commanding officer did not bother to look at us.

We followed the orderly out the front door, me breathing a sigh of relief to be out of the building. We turned right, walked along the front of the building, then turned again at the corner and started down the block. Half-way down, a loud shout stopped us in our tracks. An officer was running toward us, waving a cap in his hand. I didn't know what to think. When he caught up to us, he explained he wanted to exchange his cap for one of Sacco's NYPD caps before anyone else got the chance.

After swapping caps, the two of them embraced, now the best of friends. Sacco was delighted.

Several police cars and utility trucks were parked around the rear of the building, and the officer accompanying us crossed the street and disappeared into another building. Minutes later he reappeared with two new patches and handed them to Sacco.

Our excursion had met with more success than Sacco had hoped for, so we said goodbye and walked back up the block where Sacco asked two officers in a parked police car where we could find a cab. When he told them why we had visited the station, the officers said they would be happy to drive us back to the hotel in the squad car.

"I don't know," said Sacco, grinning at me. "What do you think the ladies would say if we arrived in a police car with these guys and their guns?"

He relished the idea, but then thought better of it. "I don't think they would appreciate it," he said. "I better tell these guys that we appreciate the offer, but we'll take a cab."

— 4 —

Later that afternoon under threatening skies we drove in taxis to the Pastoral Lourdes Retreat House, and the moment we arrived the heavens unleashed a torrential rain, dousing us as we raced for cover under trees by the entrance.

A nun welcomed us at the door, led us into a cafeteria-meeting room, explained when supper would be served, told us to make ourselves comfortable, and wished us a productive retreat.

"There's a revival meeting going on in the chapel," she said. "We hope the singing won't disturb your meeting."

With that, she left.

"There are three objectives," Sinclair said, introducing the afternoon's schedule. "First, you need time for reflection. Then we'll share responses to the Salvadoran experience. And finally, you'll need to work up plans for related activities for when you return to the university."

Earlier, Kempton, Willison, and Reid had agreed to serve on the ad hoc steering committee to work out the details.

"We'll talk over the parameters of the meeting," he said. "While we're doing that, why don't the rest of you use the time for reflection."

After a short while the planning committee broke up and we moved the chairs in a circle. Then Ventura started the meeting with a reading in Spanish of the Gospel of Mark, Chapter 4, Verses 35 to 40. Sinclair translated the verses:

The Storm on the Lake

> And he said to them on that day, when evening had come, "Let us cross over to the other side."
>
> And sending away the crowd, they took him just as he was, in the boat; and there were other boats with him.
>
> And there arose a great squall, and the waves were beating into the boat, so that the boat was now filling.
>
> And he himself was in the stern of the boat, on the cushion, asleep. And they woke him and said to him, "Master, does it not concern thee that we are perishing?"
>
> Then rising up, he rebuked the wind, and said to the sea, "Peace, be still!" And the wind fell and there came a

> great calm. And he said to them, "Why are you fearful? Are you still without faith?" And they feared exceedingly and said to one another, "Who, then, is this, that even the wind and the sea obey him?"

As Sinclair translated the passage, I wondered if the message of the gospel wasn't connected somehow to our Salvadoran experience. Could the "great squall" represent the Salvadoran civil war? And the "great calm" the promise of the peace accords? Was Christ in the gospel rebuking Salvadorans, saying, "Have faith, and all will be well"?

After Sinclair finished, he spoke a few moments about EPICA publications he thought might be of interest to the group, then Kempton and Willison filled us in on the structure for the afternoon. First, we'd try to recall a meaningful moment or experience during the trip, one that resonated for us, and share it with the group. Next, we'd discuss the larger meanings gleaned from our experiences. Then the group would draw up a list of related activities to take place after we returned to the university. Lastly we'd open the floor to discuss individual agendas.

— 5 —

Sitting in the circle, memories of what we had seen and heard flashed by in our minds as we tried our best to select an experience that held a special meaning for us.

"The moment I remember most," Reid began, "is when the young men from the Dolores Medina *carpentería* presented with us the cross. I was surprised to know that they had been preparing for us. That one moment crystallized the entire Salvadoran experience for me."

"For me," Bertsch said, "it's the spirit of the Salvadorans. They know how to survive with hope. It's an issue of faith that lives and breathes in the face of every kind of devastation. I never knew before what it meant to live under state terror. I can feel the strong presence of the spirit moving in these people."

Then Ventura's spoke up. "The behavior of Apolo moved me tremendously," he said. "He is a young man in a hurry, driven to do something for his people." Then he recalled the meeting with General Vargas. "He was really an orator, using phrases that would show his high level of training, education, and love of his country."

"He was the embodiment of the military," Gradie added, a note of irony in her voice. "A living and breathing example of the military mind."

Sacco reminisced about his meetings with Deimas during the celebrations for the war-wounded in the Central Plaza, and later at Morazán. "As we hugged, the reality of the peace accords struck me," he said.

Barker talked about the visits to the healthcare clinics. "These clinics did not resemble clinics that I had ever seen before," she said, reserving high praise for the efforts of the healthcare providers. "They are laboring under the most primitive conditions, risking their lives to care for the people."

For Willison it was the children. "Their strength and heroism under the most trying of circumstances amazes me," he said. "These children have been wounded, orphaned, and traumatized by the war. And we rarely saw any young men. They were either in the army or with the guerrillas, or they were dead."

Kempton talked about her efforts to define the term *mistica.* "I began to see the term as referring to the living church," she said, "as a sense of the Christian-based community, a sense of hope, a sense of life."

"This is a country where the truth is systematically lied about and distorted," McAllister said. "But I'm impressed with the spirit of repatriated Salvadorans. Maybe, because of that spirit, there is hope for the peace accords to succeed."

Torriera spoke about the women and children of El Salvador, and how she was excited about the Spanish Club back at school adopting the elementary school at La California. "I hope we can do something for them," she said.

For Spence, the trip to El Salvador was a chance to experience a different reality "in order to better learn one's own identity."

— 7 —

At the Retreat House, the "larger meanings" to be gleaned from our experiences were left unspoken – and for good reason. It would take months and even years for us to process those meanings.

For the time being, since from the beginnings of the trip it had been made clear that it would be our responsibility to return to campus and share the Salvadoran experience in whatever ways might benefit the school and the larger community, we agreed to come up with a list of activities to work on back at the university.

Reid started the ball rolling. "We could host a series of speakers during the coming academic year. The speakers could talk about issues raised during our visit in El Salvador."

"We could write essays on some aspect of the trip and publish them in an upcoming issue of the *Sacred Heart University Review,*" I suggested. "Not academic pieces, but more along the lines of personal responses to a place, or event, or person. The idea would be to share our experiences with the readers."

Reid, Gradie, and Barker pointed out that much of what we had learned could be integrated into our teaching to enrich the content of existing courses.

"And there is Hispanic Week at school," Torriera reminded us. "Maybe we could have a panel presentation during that week."

Then the discussion turned to finding an appropriate time to present the cross from Calle Real to the university community.

"Why not present it at the opening faculty meeting?" I asked. "You could ask for five minutes of that meeting, Jerry, describe what we did, then present the cross to Dr. Cernera."

Kempton offered another idea. "We need to develop a speaker series for our education programs," she said. "We could meet with people from local disadvantaged communities and ask them to come to SHU to speak."

Other suggestions included interviews with local community newspapers; setting up a display of enlarged photos taken during the trip to illustrate the reality of daily life in a Third World country; working on the transfer of the language lab to the National

University; forwarding books and journals to the UES; and borrowing videos from the UES to show at school.

All told, some twenty-two ideas for related activities were listed at the Retreat House.

Next it was time for "personal agendas," which meant addressing the *panadería* project for Nueva Esperanza. After a brief presentation, to my surprise, no one raised objections to the proposal, and several people donated monies on the spot. Others agreed to contribute later that evening.

While jotting down names and amounts donated in my journal, Bertsch walked over.

"How is it going?" she asked.

"We're doing fine."

"Let me know if you need more. OK?"

Finally it was time to thank Sinclair for his extraordinary efforts on our behalf. Earlier that morning after Mass, Bertsch, Ventura, and Torriera, had picked out a gift – an embroidered white cotton tunic.

"We took turns modeling the shirt to decide if it was big enough," Bertsch had said earlier. "Finally we held it up against Jose, saying, 'If it's big enough to fit Jose, it will fit Minor.'"

She handed Sinclair the shirt, and he pulled it over his head, emerging with a huge grin.

"That's really nice of you all," he said. "I really appreciate this."

"You look a little like a priest."

— 8 —

The rain stopped, and with the nuns setting up for our supper, we walked outside and filed along a path past the chapel to a large flagstone patio. In its center a giant Medusa rubber tree appeared to be standing upside down with thousands of roots shooting toward the sky, its branches curling and springing out in all directions.

Lawn chairs circled the massive trunk, a two-foot high stone wall guarded the rim of the patio, and beyond the land dropped gradually, covered by dense jungle-like vegetation with large deep russet leaves. To the right a path angled down to a terraced tropical garden and in the distance was a breathtaking view of the city.

We stood talking quietly under the branches of the tree and took in the scene, all of us coming to the realization that our trip was almost over. It was a bittersweet moment. Sinclair was right. Time was needed to digest what we had seen and heard in El Salvador. Our hearts had been broken by the testimonies we had listened to and the scenes we had witnessed, yet we also knew we had been privileged to take part in what was potentially a life-changing experience. The questions nagging all of us? Were we up to making that change? And if so, how? What form would it take? How would the lessons learned in El Salvador work themselves out in our daily lives? For example, taking Brackley's charge to us at face value: would we be willing to live up to the challenges of getting involved in social action activities with our neighbors, the poor in Bridgeport?

Sobering questions.

Back inside a long table had been set up along the rear wall and at either end smaller tables covered with blue checkerboard oilcloths, brimmed over with tortillas, plantinos, bottles of Fanta and Coke, and containers of coffee.

"The cab drivers said they would return for us at 7 o'clock," Sinclair announced, standing up. "But I don't think that's going to happen. So I have to make a few calls."

When he returned, he said he couldn't reach the cab company. "I made arrangements with the groundskeeper to drive a few of us back to the hotel. Then I'll place a call to hire cabs to drive up here to pick up the rest of you. The groundskeeper will take his wife and three passengers. So who wants to go back with me now?"

Bertsch and Torriera decided to return with Sinclair, while the rest of us would stay at the convent and wait for the cabs.

As we dined together for the last time, a mood of celebration overtook the group. We had shared a momentous experience, had resolved to participate in a series of Salvadoran-related activities back home, and had forged relationships with each other that we believed would withstand the test of time.

Someone joked about being stranded in the convent with the nuns all night. Another recalled McAllister's singing.

"Robin, it sounded really good. Could you sing it again?"

"What was I singing? I don't remember what it was."

"Frankie Lane!"

"'Ghost Riders in the Sky!'"

"'The Ballad of Sam Magee!'"

He thought for a moment, then sang several verses of the "Grey Goose" ballad. Everyone clapped and demanded more. He followed up with "The Ballad of Sam Magee."

The impromptu performance over, cards were produced and a raucous game of "Crazy 8s," punctuated with laughter and shouting, got underway.

"The nuns will be coming to tell us to shut up."

"No, they're going to throw us out of the place!"

Meanwhile, Ventura and Gradie sat off to the side, reading.

"C'mon, Charlotte," said Willison. "Let your hair down."

"No, I don't know how to play," she said. "I'll just sit here and read."

"It's easy!"

"C'mon, Jose."

"No. I don't play games."

"Charlotte, nobody knows how to play this game. It's fun."

"I'll watch," she said, putting her book down and moving over to the table.

With more coaxing, she took a seat.

"Just like one of the guys," she said, laughing.

A couple of hours later Sinclair arrived with the taxis and our time in El Salvador came to a close. And so began the start of our personal journeys . . .

EPILOGUE

The return to the States after our immersion in El Salvador was best described by Bertsch:

> It has been six weeks since our return from El Salvador. Despite several attempts to describe our journey, in anything but its most superficial aspects I have been strangely inarticulate. An unusual longing for silence has overtaken me. Tears come easily. The *New York Times* is unopened, the television silent. Time spent puttering, tending to flowers, observing the never-ending fluttering of birds at their feeders, listening to the gentle lap of waves in the Sound, have replaced my usual daily routine. . . . Slowly, recognition that I am in mourning began to move its way through the encasing silence.[15]

That mourning, that sense of physical pain and mental anguish, would last for days, months, and beyond.

"Nobody returns from a trip to El Salvador without experiencing life changes," Fr. Blanchard had prophesied in his talk to us on campus. "The spirit of the people will affect you in ways you would never expect."

It was true.

NOTES

1. James LeMoyne,"Out of the Jungle in El Salvador: Rebels with a New Cause," *New York Times Magazine (*February 9, 1992), 24 ff.

2. Dean Brackley, S.J., "The University and the 'Broken Heart' Experience," *Sacred Heart University Review* 13, nos. 1 & 2 (Fall 1992/Spring 1993), 2.

3. "Death Squad Issues Written Threat," *Centroamérica: The Monthly Review* 7, no. 11 (November 1992), 2.

4. "Five Killed, Mirna Anaya Attacked," *Centroamérica: The Monthly Review* 8, no. 2 (February 1993), 3.

5. Carolyn Forché, "The Colonel," in *The Country Between Us* (New York: HarperCollins, 1981), 16.

6. J.M. Ventura, "El Salvador – Present and Future," *Sacred Heart University Review* 12, nos. 1 & 2 (Fall 1991/Spring 1992), 26.

7. Anne M. Barker, "Health Care in El Salvador," *Sacred Heart University Review* 12, nos. 1 & 2 (Fall 1991/Spring 1992), 24.

8. Gerald Reid, "The Cross of Calle Real," *Sacred Heart University Review* 12, nos. 1 & 2 (Fall 1991/Spring 1992), 14.

9. Reid, "The Cross of Calle Real," 16.

10. Ventura, "El Salvador – Present and Future," 28.

11. Robin McAllister, "Searching for Truth in a World of Lies," *Sacred Heart University Review* 12, nos. 1 & 2 (Fall 1991/Spring 1992), 36.

12. Eilene Bertsch, "Beyond Death and Destruction – Faith and Hope," *Sacred Heart University Review* 12, nos. 1 & 2 (Fall 1991/Spring 1992), 7.

13. Bertsch, "Beyond Death and Destruction," 7.

14. Bertsch, "Beyond Death and Destruction," 5.

15. Bertsch, "Beyond Death and Destruction," 4.

GLOSSARY

Attacatl Battalion. Deriving its name from an historical Salvadoran indigenous warrior, the Atlacatl Battalion was one of five rapid-reaction units backed by American aid at the start of the civil war. Created in 1980 and trained in anti-guerrilla operations by American advisors at the U.S. Army's School of the Americas, the battalion was deployed back to El Salvador in 1981 to turn around a losing ground war. The Atlacatl took part in the 1981 massacre of at least 794 peasants and children in the El Mozote, and later, members of the battalion were implicated in the 1989 murder of six Jesuits, their housekeeper and her daughter, at the University of Central America (UCA). The battalion was headed by the charismatic field commander, Domingo Monterrosa.

Roberto d' Aubuisson. A rightist leader, former National Guard officer, and one of the founders of the Nationalist Republican Alliance (ARENA), d'Aubuisson ran for the presidency of El Salvador in 1984, and was defeated by José Napoleón Duarte. He founded the Union of White Warriors, a death squad implicated in many murders, and according to the Truth Commission, planned and ordered the assassination of Archbishop Oscar Arnulfo Romero in 1980. Associated with hard-line radical rightists, he led his party's efforts to stall land reform. Robert E. White, the U.S. ambassador to El Salvador from 1977 to 1980 called d'Aubisson a "pathological killer."

CARITAS (Charity). Founded in Germany in 1897, CARITAS shares the mission of the Catholic Church to serve the poor and promote charity and justice throughout the world. The international organization made up of more than 160 national charitable groups currently serves seven regions (Africa, Asia, Europe, Latin America and the Caribbean, the Middle East and North Africa, North America, and Oceania).

Christian Urgent Action Network on Emergency Support (CUANES). The network reported on Salvadoran Army human rights abuses of religious workers in Christian communities perceived to be supportive of Salvadoran guerrillas. Abuses included deportation, harassment, and the disappearing of individuals.

Committee of Mothers and Relatives of Political Prisoners, Disappeared, and Assassinated of El Salvador (COMADRES). Founded in 1977 with the help of the Archdiocese of San Salvador and Archbishop Oscar Romero, the women of COMADRES organized to free political prisoners and discover what happened to the disappeared. The organization, praised by the international community, was subject to government raids, and members were tortured and assassinated by death squads.

COPAZ (National Commission to Consolidate Peace). This United Nations Commission was tasked with monitoring the compliance of the full demobilization of Salvadoran warring factions stipulated by the peace accords. The commission's central aims were to assure the agreed upon stages of disarmament, support a generous program of land redistribution, and push for social and economic transformation.

CRISPAZ (Christians for Peace in El Salvador). Begun in 1984 in response to the havoc of the Salvadoran civil war, this organization continues working with churches in El Salvador. Its mission statement reads: "CRISPAZ is a faith-based organization dedicated to building bridges of solidarity between the Church of the poor and marginalized communities in El Salvador and communities in the U.S. and other countries through mutual accompaniment, striving together for peace, justice, sustainability, and human liberation."

Death Squads. Current and formerembers of the military and police forces, opposed to the tactics of the FMLN and convinced that El Salvador was in danger of falling into the hands of leftist terrorists, formed paramilitary squads that "disappeared" and murdered adversaries, leaving mutilated corpses along roads and often prominently displayed in public places. Using unmarked cars with darkened windows, they abducted, tortured, and killed opposition leaders and suspected guerilla sympathizers, terrorizing the populace.

Doctors Without Borders. This international organization was founded by doctors in France in 1971 and provides high-quality medical care to populations threatened by violence, armed conflict, epidemics, and natural disasters.

Ecumenical Program in Central America and the Caribbean (EPICA). An organization combating socio-economic injustice, the marginalization of the poor, and military repression in Latin America, EPICA advocates solidarity with the poor and disenfranchised. It conducts study tours to oppressed communities, publishes books on issues affecting people subjugated by military and government structures, and emphasizes spiritual reflection and social action. Sacred Heart University faculty tours to El Salvador were organized and led by members of EPICA.

El Mozote. A village in northern Morazán, El Mozote, was the site in December 1981 of a brutal massacre that left an entire village decimated, with over seven hundred men, women, and children slaughtered by the Atlacatl battalion of the Salvadoran military. In the December 6, 1993 edition of the *New Yorker*, Mark Danner provides a blow-by-blow account based on extensive investigative reporting of the buildup to the massacre, what took place during the slaughter, and the following cover-up by Salvadoran and U.S. governments. El Mozote became a rallying cry, swelling the ranks of the insurgents, and fueling the early opposition of the international community to the war.

El Rescate. This human rights group was founded in California in 1981 to respond to the plight of refugees fleeing to the U.S. from the Salvadoran war. Over a thirty-year period, the group has served more than half a million people, and conducted a study of military abuses used by the Truth Commission to purge Salvadoran officer ranks.

El Salvador's Civil War. Christine J. Wade offers a succinct overview of the roots of El Salvador's civil war in her article "El Salvador: A Contradiction of Neoliberalism and Building Sustainable Peace." She writes:

> There are four key developments in Salvadoran history that contributed to the onset of civil war. First, the seizure of communal lands to promote coffee exports resulted in an extreme concentration of wealth and high rates of landlessness. Second, the economic and political crisis of the 1930s resulted in the installation of a military regime, which promoted the interests of the coffee elite. This alliance between the military and the oligarchy would dominate Salvadoran society for the next 60 years. Third, the period from 1948 to 1979 is characterized by cycles of repression and reform by successive military governments in an attempt to either control or placate the population. Finally, when the electoral opposition posed a serious threat to the interests of the status quo in 1972 and 1977, the electoral option was withdrawn and violence was used to control or stop dissent. The systematic use of repression reduced, and eventually eliminated, political space for the opposition. This realization led to a dramatic increase in the number of radical popular organizations in El Salvador, an increase that was met by unprecedented levels of violence. Increasing repression combined with a deteriorating economy proved to be a volatile combination. In El Salvador, the combination of the collapse of political space and socio-economic inequalities were key factors contributing to the war. (*International Journal of Peace Studies* 13, no. 2 [Autumn/Winter 2008], 19)

FMLN (Frente Farabundo Martí para la Liberación Nacional). In 1980 five left-wing groups sympathetic to the causes of Salvadoran peasants united to liberate the country from the power-elites and the repressive tactics of right-wing government forces. Their organization was named after the leader of an anti-military government uprising in El Salvador in 1932. Filling its ranks with Marxists, radicalized priests, organized *campesinos,* trade unionists, and angry students, the FMLN waged a guerrilla war with growing success during the twelve-year campaign, controlling much of the provinces of Morazán and Chalatenango. With UN and strong international backing the guerrillas forced the government to the bargaining table to sign the peace accords in January 1992. After the war, despite escalating differences among its leaders, the FMLN succeeded in becoming part of the emerging political landscape, electing officials throughout the country and winning the presidency in 2009 and again in 2014.

The Four Churchwomen. On December 2, 1980, four American missionary women were abducted, raped, and murdered by a National Guard death squad at Santiago Nonualco, El Salvador. Maryknoll sisters Maura Clarke and Ita Ford, Ursuline nun Dorothy Kazel, and Jean Donovan, a laywoman, were on a Catholic relief mission when attacked. Four National Guard soldiers, who years later said they were acting on orders of superiors, were convicted in 1984 of the murders and received prison terms of 30 years. Robert White, American ambassador to El Salvador when the killings occurred, later said, "It is totally outrageous" to let "the intellectual authors of this terrible incident off scot free" (*New York Times,* April 3, 1998, A-12).

The Fourteen Families of El Salvador. From its early history, dozens of wealthy elites controlled much the coffee-producing lands in the fourteen departments (regions) of El Salvador. Supported by repressive legislatures and the military, the families appropriated the most productive lands, leaving the remainder to poor subsistence farmers. The resulting tensions between the wealthy and the *campesinos* gave rise to the MATANZA (see below), and in the late 1970s to the start of the brutal civil war.

La Matanza (The Slaughter). This 1932 massacre took place in the western departments of El Salvador, and left 10,000 to 40,000 Salvadoran peasants dead, including among others the leftist leader Agustin Farabundo Martí. After staging a successful coup in December of 1931, General Maximiliano Heránandez Martínez, led a better trained and equipped Salvadoran Army against the leftist uprising, specifically targeting the indigenous population.

Liberation Theology. This school of thought interprets the gospel teachings of Jesus Christ as a call to action to liberate the poor and oppressed from unjust social, political, and economic structures. Its founder, Gustavo Gutiérrez, outlined the basic tenets of the movement in *A Theology of Liberation,* espousing the "preferential option for the poor," one of the basic principles of Catholic social teaching in the twentieth century.

Maquiladoras. Operating in Free Trade Zones, these factories hire low-paid young women to work long hours sewing and assembling products for the Gap, J.C. Penney, Levi Strauss, and others that are then sold on the American market. Bob Herbert, in an Op-Ed article for the *New York Times* wrote, "The Free Trade Zones in which the sweatshops flourish in Central America and the Caribbean were promoted by the U.S. Government and largely financed by U.S. taxpayers. They are a scandal." He cited "a glossy full-color ad" aimed at clothing executives in a major trade magazine featuring "a young woman seated at a sewing machine in a shirt factory. . . . *You* can hire her for 33 cents an hour" ("Sweatshop Beneficiaries," July 24, 1995, A 13).

National Civil Police (PNC). Created in 1992, the National Civil Police are responsible for maintaining order and public security in El Salvador. Under the UN-sponsored accords, the National Police, the Treasury Police, and the National Guard (formerly part of the Salvadoran armed forces), were disbanded because of involvement in human rights violations, and replaced by the PNC under civilian control. "All together, these units have been responsible for the torture, disappearance or death of tens of thousands of civilians," wrote Dean Brackley in "Peace for El Salvador" (*America,* February 22, 1992, 131). Members of the newly formed PNC were to be recruited in equal numbers from the government police forces and FMLN guerrillas.

Nationalist Republican Alliance (ARENA). Roberto d'Aubuisson formed the right-wing ARENA party in 1981 in response to the growing insurgency movement in the country. Characterized by a strong anti-communist agenda, the party won the support of U.S. officials, and paved the way for a U.S.-backed financing of the war and the training of Salvadoran government military forces. The party controlled the National Assembly until 1985, and its presidential candidate Alfredo Cristiani won election in 1989. During the postwar years, despite gains by FMLN candidates, the party continued to win elections until 2012 when Anthony Saca, then president, was expelled from the party for suspected widespread corruption.

Neoliberalism. This political philosophy champions open markets, free trade, and the reduced role of government control over the economy. After the civil war the right-wing ARENA governing party in El Salvador espoused neoliberal economic policies that critics believe exacerbated inequality and poverty and threatened the future success of the peace accords.

Non-Governmental Human Rights Commission of El Salvador (CDHES). An early human rights information project that between 1977 and 1990 collected over 9,000 testimonies on abuses during the twelve year civil war. Its findings were instrumental in removing human rights abusers from the ranks of the military.

People's Revolutionary Army (ERP). One of five groups comprising the FMLN, the Peoples' Revolutionary Army, led by the guerrilla tactician Joaquín Villalobos, fought the Salvadoran army to a standstill in the latter part of the 1980s. During the demobilization period following the civil war, Villalobos and his supporters harbored concerns about the reorganization of the Salvadoran Army, the purge of its officers cited for human rights violations, and the distribution of land to the guerillas, but supported the end of hostilities and the integration of the FMLN into the national political landscape. "We are aware that we made errors," said Villalobos in a February 1992 speech, "that we were not infallible and that this is the moment to say to the nation, with humility, that we recognize this. We do not care if the errors of others were greater or lesser than ours, or if they will recognize them some day. We are convinced that without truth and justice, we have neither reconciliation nor peace" (quoted in "Peace for El Salvador," *America,* February 1992, 133).

Recalendarization. Compliance with the stipulations of the peace accords calling for a purge of senior Salvadoran military officers and the demobilization of rebel forces by October 31, 1992, met with failure. Amid escalating tensions threatening the breakdown of the cease-fire (including reports of an army-planned coup d'état*),* and under intense UN pressure, President Alfredo Cristiani agreed to implement the "purification" of the army, and Joaquín Villalobos, military leader of the insurgents, accepted the mandate for full demobilization of rebel ranks by December 15. The new date was hailed as signaling the "end of the war."

Rerum Novarum. This encyclical issued by Leo XIII on May 15, 1991, on the "condition of Labor," spelled out a modern-day version of the rights to property, the relations between employers and workers, the rights of workers to organize for their mutual benefit, and the employee's right to remuneration "sufficient to maintain the wage-earner in reasonable and frugal comfort." *Rerum Novarum* has been lauded for espousing the principles of industrial justice.

School of the Americas (SOA). Established in 1946 in Panama by the U.S. Department of Defense, the SOA, called the "School of the Americas' Assassins" by its detractors, provided anti-communist counterinsurgency training for Central American army personnel.

In the late 1970s and early 1980s, the school trained the Salvadoran Atlacatyl Battalion, the unit responsible for the El Mozote massacre and the assassination of the UCA Jesuits. Transferred to Fort Benning, Georgia in 1984, the SOA became increasingly criticized for the human rights violations of its graduates that included enhanced interrogation techniques, extortion, kidnapping, and executions. Public protests and demonstrations calling for the school to shut its doors prompted its renaming in 2007 as the Western Hemisphere Institute for Security Cooperation.

Solidarity. This term is used in El Salvador and elsewhere in the world to describe a "joining together" of "the haves" with marginalized people to seek social, economic, and political change. Solidarity, a key ingredient of liberation theology and its message of the "preferential option for the poor," calls for listening to the stories of the oppressed, and coming to an understanding what it means to be non-participants in life: to be hungry, illiterate, and exploited by others. Solidarity demands dialog so that the non-poor begin questioning the structures in place that serve to oppress the less fortunate. Finally being "in solidarity" calls for "the haves" and the marginalized working together to become agents of change.

Truth Commission. The 1992 UN-brokered peace accords established a Truth Commission for El Salvador to investigate human rights violations during the twelve-year civil war. The full report, *From Madness to Hope: The 12-Year War in El Salvador. Report of the Commission on the Truth for El Salvador* (United Nations Security Council, April 1, 1993, S/25500), offers a detailed history of the war, uncovers the truth about specific incidents in the war, and names those who ordered and/or carried out atrocities. After extensive research and examination of thousands of testimonies, the commission report, seeking to assign responsibility for thousands of deaths, blamed the government and right-wing death squads for the bulk of human rights atrocities, and called for the dismissal of senior Salvadoran military officers, changes in the country's judicial system, further investigations into the activities of the death squads, and asserted that American officials arguing for continued U.S. support of the war were misinformed or cynical about what had occurred in the country.

United Nations Observers Mission in El Salvador (ONUSAL). This mission played a key role in the Salvadoran peace process by mediating negotiations that led to the peace accords. The mission oversaw the implementation of the accords, including monitoring human rights violations, the demobilization of the FMLN rebel army, and the reorganization of the Salvadoran armed forces.

U.S. Involvement in Salvadoran Civil War. In an effort to contain the spread of Communism and its ideology throughout Central America, the U.S. supported the Salvadoran military in its fight against the Marxist guerrillas of the FMLN by supplying intelligence gathering, strategic planning, and training officers and foot soldiers. Clifford Krauss wrote, "Between 1979 and 1992, the Carter, Reagan and Bush Administrations poured more than $6 billion into El Salvador to modernize the Army and defeat the guerrillas. Critics of the policy have long accused Washington of being implicated in the slaughter of thousands by looking the other way when its allies committed crimes" (*New York Times,* Washington, March 15, 1993, A 12). In an Op-Ed column, Anthony Lewis wrote that the U.S. supported "a Salvadoran Government that was dominated by killers. We armed them, trained their soldiers and covered up their crimes" (*New York Times,* March 22, 1993, A 17).